THE GOSPEL ACCORDING TO
ST. JOHN

TODAY'S ENGLISH VERSION ✛

CHRIST IN MAJESTY WITH SYMBOLS OF THE EVANGELISTS

THE GOSPEL ACCORDING TO
ST. JOHN

TODAY'S ENGLISH VERSION ✛

AMERICAN BIBLE SOCIETY
NEW YORK

The Gospel According to John

Imprimatur:
✠Most Reverend William H. Keeler, D. D.
President, National Conference of
Catholic Bishops

March 10, 1993

Front cover art: St. John the Evangelist, The British
Library / Art Resource, NY

Frontispiece: The British Library

ISBN 1-58516-187-X

Printed in the United States of America
Eng. Port. TEV560P-109880
ABS-8/00-3,000—CG1

FOREWORD

The Good News Bible in *Today's English Version* is a new translation which seeks to state clearly and accurately the meaning of the original texts in words and forms that are widely accepted by people who use English as a means of communication. This translation does not follow the traditional vocabulary and style found in the historic English Bible versions. Rather it attempts in this century to set forth the biblical content and message in the standard, everyday, natural form of English.

The aim of this Bible is to give today's reader maximum understanding of the content of the original texts. The preface explains the nature of special aids for readers which are included in the volume. It also sets forth the basic principles which translators followed in their work.

The Bible in *Today's English Version* was translated and published by the United Bible Societies for use throughout the world. The Bible Societies trust that the reading and study of this translation will result in a better understanding of the meaning of the Bible. We also earnestly pray that readers will discover the message of saving faith and hope for all people which the Bible contains.

Introduction to the Gospels

The Gospels provide various pictures of the life and teachings of Jesus Christ. The word "Gospel" comes from an Old English word that means "good news." The Greek word that is translated as "gospel" or "good news" is *euangelion* (see MARK 1.1). The English words "evangelist" and "evangelism" come from this word. An evangelist is one who tells good news.

The Gospels (Matthew, Mark, Luke, and John) were probably written down in their present form between 30 and 60 years after Jesus died and was raised to life by God. Since Jesus himself left no writings, the Gospels record stories and eyewitness descriptions that had been passed on by word of mouth for a number of years. At first, Jesus' followers were so eager to tell the message about him that they didn't think it was necessary to write down what he had said and done. But as Jesus' first followers and eyewitnesses grew older and died, it became more important to have a written record of Jesus and his teachings, and to describe his death and how God brought him back to life.

Although other "gospels" were written, the only ones accepted as reliable by the whole church were MATTHEW, MARK, LUKE, and JOHN. It is not certain who actually wrote the Gospels, since the names of the authors are never given in the books that bear the names of MATTHEW, MARK, LUKE, and JOHN. The Gospels were probably written between A.D. 60, ten years before the temple was destroyed in Jerusalem, and A.D.100. Most scholars agree that MARK was most likely the first Gospel written, since MATTHEW and LUKE seem to take many of their details and the order of events directly from MARK.

Many sources were used to create the Gospels. These probably included various collections of Jesus' sayings and stories that were available to the Gospel writers. For example, a number of Jesus' sayings are similar in MATTHEW and LUKE, so they may have been working with the same source. They also appear to have used MARK for their basic outlines. But MATTHEW and LUKE used different sources to describe the events surrounding Jesus' birth, since MARK begins after Jesus is already grown up. Because MATTHEW, MARK, and LUKE have so much material in common and follow the same basic outline, they are sometimes referred to as the "Synoptic" Gospels (from the Greek word synopsis, which means "seeing together").

These Synoptic Gospels are more like each other than any of them is like the Gospel of JOHN. While MATTHEW, MARK, and LUKE focus on Jesus' public teaching and miracle working in Galilee, JOHN contains information about Jesus' early work in Judea. These include the so-called "I am" sayings, such as "I am the bread that gives life!" (JOHN 6.35); "I am the light for the world!" (John 8.12); and many more. The order of events in JOHN does not follow the order shared by MATTHEW, MARK, and LUKE. And JOHN does not include any of Jesus' stories (parables) that are found in the other three Gospels. Each Gospel presents its own perspective on the events of Jesus' life and his teachings. For more about what makes each of these accounts of Jesus' life and ministry unique, see the Introduction to each Gospel.

The Gospel according to
JOHN

INTRODUCTION

The Gospel according to John presents Jesus as the eternal Word of God, who "became a human being and lived among us." As the book itself says, this Gospel was written so that its readers might believe that Jesus is the promised Savior, the Son of God, and that through their faith in him they may have life (20.31).

After an introduction that identifies the eternal Word of God with Jesus, the first part of the Gospel presents various miracles which show that Jesus is the promised Savior, the Son of God. These are followed by discourses that explain what is revealed by the miracles. This part of the book tells how some people believed in Jesus and became his followers, while others opposed him and refused to believe. Chapters 13–17 record at length the close fellowship of Jesus with his disciples on the night of his arrest, and his words of preparation and encouragement to them on the eve of his crucifixion. The closing chapters tell of Jesus' arrest and trial, his crucifixion and resurrection, and his appearances to his disciples after the resurrection.

The story of the woman caught in adultery (8.1-11) is placed in brackets because many manuscripts and early translations omit it, while others include it in other places.

John emphasizes the gift of eternal life through Christ, a gift which begins now and which comes to those who respond to Jesus as the way, the truth, and the life. A striking feature of *John* is the symbolic use of common things from everyday life to point to spiritual realities, such as water, bread, light, the shepherd and his sheep, and the grapevine and its fruit.

OUTLINE OF CONTENTS

The Word of Life

1 In the beginning the Word already existed; the Word was with God, and the Word was God. ² From the very beginning the Word was with God. ³ Through him God made all things; not one thing in all creation was made without him. ⁴ The Word was the source of life,^{a} and this life brought light to people. ⁵ The light shines in the

---

^{a} The Word was the source of life; *or* What was made had life in union with the Word.

darkness, and the darkness has never put it out.

⁶God sent his messenger, a man named John, ⁷who came to tell people about the light, so that all should hear the message and believe. ⁸He himself was not the light; he came to tell about the light. ⁹This was the real light — the light that comes into the world and shines on all people.

¹⁰The Word was in the world, and though God made the world through him, yet the world did not recognize him. ¹¹He came to his own country, but his own people did not receive him. ¹²Some, however, did receive him and believed in him; so he gave them the right to become God's children. ¹³They did not become God's children by natural means, that is, by being born as the children of a human father; God himself was their Father.

¹⁴The Word became a human being and, full of grace and truth, lived among us. We saw his glory, the glory which he received as the Father's only Son.

¹⁵John spoke about him. He cried out, "This is the one I was talking about when I said, 'He comes after me, but he is greater than I am, because he existed before I was born.' "

¹⁶Out of the fullness of his grace he has blessed us all, giving us one blessing after another. ¹⁷God gave the Law through Moses, but grace and truth came through Jesus Christ. ¹⁸No one has ever seen God. The only Son, who is the same as God and is at the Father's side, he has made him known.

John the Baptist's Message
(Matthew 3.1-12; Mark 1.1-8;
Luke 3.1-18)

¹⁹The Jewish authorities in Jerusalem sent some priests and Levites to John to ask him, "Who are you?"

²⁰John did not refuse to answer, but spoke out openly and clearly, saying: "I am not the Messiah."

²¹"Who are you, then?" they asked. "Are you Elijah?"

"No, I am not," John answered.

"Are you the Prophet?"ᵇ they asked.

"No," he replied.

²²"Then tell us who you are," they said. "We have to take an answer back to those who sent us. What do you say about yourself?"

²³John answered by quoting the prophet Isaiah:

"I am 'the voice of someone
    shouting in the desert:
Make a straight path for the
    Lord to travel!' "

²⁴The messengers, who had been sent by the Pharisees, ²⁵thenᶜ asked John, "If you are not the Messiah nor Elijah nor the Prophet, why do you baptize?"

²⁶John answered, "I baptize with water, but among you stands the one you do not know. ²⁷He is coming after me, but I am not good enough even to untie his sandals."

²⁸All this happened in Bethany on the east side of the Jordan River, where John was baptizing.

The Lamb of God

²⁹The next day John saw Jesus coming to him, and said, "There is the Lamb of God, who takes away the sin of the world! ³⁰This is the one I was talking about when I said, 'A man is coming

---

ᵇ THE PROPHET: *The one who was expected to appear and announce the coming of the Messiah.*   ᶜ The messengers, who had been sent by the Pharisees, then; *or* Those who had been sent were Pharisees; they.

1.6 Mt 3.1; Mk 1.4; Lk 3.1, 2   **1.21 a** Ml 4.5; **b** Dt 18.15, 18   **1.23** Is 40.3 (LXX)

after me, but he is greater than I am, because he existed before I was born.' 31 I did not know who he would be, but I came baptizing with water in order to make him known to the people of Israel."

32 And John gave this testimony: "I saw the Spirit come down like a dove

I saw the Spirit come down like a dove. (1.32)

from heaven and stay on him. 33 I still did not know that he was the one, but God, who sent me to baptize with water, had said to me, 'You will see the Spirit come down and stay on a man; he is the one who baptizes with the Holy Spirit.' 34 I have seen it," said John, "and I tell you that he is the Son of God."

The First Disciples of Jesus

35 The next day John was standing there again with two of his disciples, 36 when he saw Jesus walking by. "There is the Lamb of God!" he said.

37 The two disciples heard him say this and went with Jesus. 38 Jesus turned, saw them following him, and asked, "What are you looking for?"

They answered, "Where do you live, Rabbi?" (This word means "Teacher.")

39 "Come and see," he answered. (It was then about four o'clock in the afternoon.) So they went with him and saw where he lived, and spent the rest of that day with him.

40 One of them was Andrew, Simon Peter's brother. 41 At once he found his brother Simon and told him, "We have found the Messiah." (This word means "Christ.") 42 Then he took Simon to Jesus.

Jesus looked at him and said, "Your name is Simon son of John, but you will be called Cephas." (This is the same as Peter and means "a rock.")

Jesus Calls Philip and Nathanael

43 The next day Jesus decided to go to Galilee. He found Philip and said to him, "Come with me!" (44 Philip was from Bethsaida, the town where Andrew and Peter lived.) 45 Philip found Nathanael and told him, "We have found the one whom Moses wrote about in the book of the Law and whom the prophets also wrote about. He is Jesus son of Joseph, from Nazareth."

46 "Can anything good come from Nazareth?" Nathanael asked.

"Come and see," answered Philip.

47 When Jesus saw Nathanael coming to him, he said about him, "Here is a real Israelite; there is nothing false in him!"

48 Nathanael asked him, "How do you know me?"

Jesus answered, "I saw you when you were under the fig tree before Philip called you."

49 "Teacher," answered Nathanael, "you are the Son of God! You are the King of Israel!"

50 Jesus said, "Do you believe just because I told you I saw you when you were under the fig tree? You will see much greater things than this!" 51 And he said to them, "I am telling you the truth: you will see heaven open and

1.51 Gn 28.12

God's angels going up and coming down on the Son of Man."

The Wedding in Cana

2 Two days later there was a wedding in the town of Cana in Galilee. Jesus' mother was there, ²and Jesus and his disciples had also been invited to the wedding. ³When the wine had given out, Jesus' mother said to him, "They are out of wine."

⁴"You must not tell me what to do," Jesus replied. "My time has not yet come."

⁵Jesus' mother then told the servants, "Do whatever he tells you."

⁶The Jews have rules about ritual washing, and for this purpose six stone water jars were there, each one large enough to hold between twenty and thirty gallons. ⁷Jesus said to the servants, "Fill these jars with water." They

"Fill these jars with water." (2.7)

filled them to the brim, ⁸and then he told them, "Now draw some water out and take it to the man in charge of the feast." They took him the water, ⁹which now had turned into wine, and he tasted it. He did not know where this wine had come from (but, of course, the servants who had drawn out the water

knew); so he called the bridegroom ¹⁰and said to him, "Everyone else serves the best wine first, and after the guests have drunk a lot, he serves the ordinary wine. But you have kept the best wine until now!"

¹¹Jesus performed this first miracle in Cana in Galilee; there he revealed his glory, and his disciples believed in him.

¹²After this, Jesus and his mother, brothers, and disciples went to Capernaum and stayed there a few days.

Jesus Goes to the Temple
(Matthew 21.12, 13; Mark 11.15-17; Luke 19.45, 46)

¹³It was almost time for the Passover Festival, so Jesus went to Jerusalem. ¹⁴There in the Temple he found people selling cattle, sheep, and pigeons, and also the moneychangers sitting at their tables. ¹⁵So he made a whip from cords and drove all the animals out of the Temple, both the sheep and the cattle; he overturned the tables of the moneychangers and scattered their coins; ¹⁶and he ordered those who sold the pigeons, "Take them out of here! Stop making my Father's house a marketplace!" ¹⁷His disciples remembered that the scripture says, "My devotion to your house, O God, burns in me like a fire."

¹⁸The Jewish authorities came back at him with a question, "What miracle can you perform to show us that you have the right to do this?"

¹⁹Jesus answered, "Tear down this Temple, and in three days I will build it again."

²⁰"Are you going to build it again in three days?" they asked him. "It has taken forty-six years to build this Temple!"

²¹But the temple Jesus was speaking about was his body. ²²So when he was raised from death, his disciples remembered that he had said this, and they

---

2.12 Mt 4.13   **2.13** Ex 12.1-27   **2.17** Ps 69.9   **2.19** Mt 26.61; 27.40; Mk 14.58; 15.29

believed the scripture and what Jesus had said.

Jesus' Knowledge of Human Nature

²³While Jesus was in Jerusalem during the Passover Festival, many believed in him as they saw the miracles he performed. ²⁴But Jesus did not trust himself to them, because he knew them all. ²⁵There was no need for anyone to tell him about them, because he himself knew what was in their hearts.

Jesus and Nicodemus

3 There was a Jewish leader named Nicodemus, who belonged to the party of the Pharisees. ²One night he went to Jesus and said to him, "Rabbi, we know that you are a teacher sent by God. No one could perform the miracles you are doing unless God were with him."

³Jesus answered, "I am telling you the truth: no one can see the Kingdom of God without being born again."ᵈ

⁴"How can a grown man be born again?" Nicodemus asked. "He certainly cannot enter his mother's womb and be born a second time!"

⁵"I am telling you the truth," replied Jesus, "that no one can enter the Kingdom of God without being born of water and the Spirit. ⁶A person is born physically of human parents, but is born spiritually of the Spirit. ⁷Do not be surprised because I tell you that you must all be born again.ᵈ ⁸The wind blows wherever it wishes; you hear the sound it makes, but you do not know where it comes from or where it is going. It is like that with everyone who is born of the Spirit."

⁹"How can this be?" asked Nicodemus.

¹⁰Jesus answered, "You are a great teacher in Israel, and you don't know this? ¹¹I am telling you the truth: we speak of what we know and report what we have seen, yet none of you is willing to accept our message. ¹²You do not believe me when I tell you about the things of this world; how will you ever believe me, then, when I tell you about the things of heaven? ¹³And no one has ever gone up to heaven except the Son of Man, who came down from heaven."ᵉ

¹⁴As Moses lifted up the bronze snake on a pole in the desert, in the same way the Son of Man must be lifted up, ¹⁵so that everyone who believes in him may have eternal life. ¹⁶For God loved the world so much that he gave his only Son, so that everyone who believes in him may not die but have eternal life. ¹⁷For God did not send his Son into the world to be its judge, but to be its savior.

¹⁸Those who believe in the Son are not judged; but those who do not believe have already been judged, because they have not believed in God's only Son. ¹⁹This is how the judgment works: the light has come into the world, but people love the darkness rather than the light, because their deeds are evil. ²⁰Those who do evil things hate the light and will not come to the light, because they do not want their evil deeds to be shown up. ²¹But those who do what is true come to the light in order that the light may show that what they did was in obedience to God.

Jesus and John

²²After this, Jesus and his disciples went to the province of Judea, where he spent some time with them and baptized. ²³John also was baptizing in Ae-

---

ᵈ again; or from above.   ᵉ The quotation may continue through verse 21.
3.14 Nu 21.9

non, not far from Salim, because there was plenty of water in that place. People were going to him, and he was baptizing them. (24 This was before John had been put in prison.)

25 Some of John's disciples began arguing with a Jew*f* about the matter of ritual washing. 26 So they went to John and told him, "Teacher, you remember the man who was with you on the east side of the Jordan, the one you spoke about? Well, he is baptizing now, and everyone is going to him!"

27 John answered, "No one can have anything unless God gives it. 28 You yourselves are my witnesses that I said, 'I am not the Messiah, but I have been sent ahead of him.' 29 The bridegroom is the one to whom the bride belongs; but the bridegroom's friend, who stands by and listens, is glad when he hears the bridegroom's voice. This is how my own happiness is made complete. 30 He must become more important while I become less important."

He Who Comes from Heaven

31 He who comes from above is greater than all. He who is from the earth belongs to the earth and speaks about earthly matters, but he who comes from heaven is above all. 32 He tells what he has seen and heard, yet no one accepts his message. 33 But whoever accepts his message confirms by this that God is truthful. 34 The one whom God has sent speaks God's words, because God gives him the fullness of his Spirit. 35 The Father loves his Son and has put everything in his power. 36 Whoever believes in the Son has eternal life; whoever disobeys the Son will not have life, but will remain under God's punishment.

Jesus and the Samaritan Woman

4 The Pharisees heard that Jesus was winning and baptizing more disciples than John. (2 Actually, Jesus himself did not baptize anyone; only his disciples did.) 3 So when Jesus heard what was being said, he left Judea and went back to Galilee; 4 on his way there he had to go through Samaria.

5 In Samaria he came to a town named Sychar, which was not far from the field that Jacob had given to his son Joseph. 6 Jacob's well was there, and Jesus, tired out by the trip, sat down by the well. It was about noon.

7 A Samaritan woman came to draw some water, and Jesus said to her, "Give

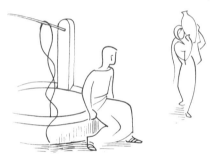

"Give me a drink of water." (4.7)

me a drink of water." (8 His disciples had gone into town to buy food.)

9 The woman answered, "You are a Jew, and I am a Samaritan — so how can you ask me for a drink?" (Jews will not use the same cups and bowls that Samaritans use.)*g*

10 Jesus answered, "If you only knew what God gives and who it is that is asking you for a drink, you would ask him, and he would give you life-giving water."

11 "Sir," the woman said, "you don't have a bucket, and the well is deep.

---

f a Jew; *some manuscripts have* some Jews.   *g* Jews will not use the same cups and bowls that Samaritans use; *or* Jews will have nothing to do with Samaritans.
3.24 Mt 14.3; Mk 6.17; Lk 3.19, 20   **3.28** Jn 1.20   **3.35** Mt 11.27; Lk 10.22
4.5 Gn 33.19; Js 24.32   **4.9** Ezra 4.1-5; Ne 4.1, 2

Where would you get that life-giving water? ¹²It was our ancestor Jacob who gave us this well; he and his children and his flocks all drank from it. You don't claim to be greater than Jacob, do you?"

¹³Jesus answered, "Those who drink this water will get thirsty again, ¹⁴but those who drink the water that I will give them will never be thirsty again. The water that I will give them will become in them a spring which will provide them with life-giving water and give them eternal life."

¹⁵"Sir," the woman said, "give me that water! Then I will never be thirsty again, nor will I have to come here to draw water."

¹⁶"Go and call your husband," Jesus told her, "and come back."

¹⁷"I don't have a husband," she answered.

Jesus replied, "You are right when you say you don't have a husband. ¹⁸You have been married to five men, and the man you live with now is not really your husband. You have told me the truth."

¹⁹"I see you are a prophet, sir," the woman said. ²⁰"My Samaritan ancestors worshiped God on this mountain, but you Jews say that Jerusalem is the place where we should worship God."

²¹Jesus said to her, "Believe me, woman, the time will come when people will not worship the Father either on this mountain or in Jerusalem. ²²You Samaritans do not really know whom you worship; but we Jews know whom we worship, because it is from the Jews that salvation comes. ²³But the time is coming and is already here, when by the power of God's Spirit people will worship the Father as he really is, offering him the true worship that he wants. ²⁴God is Spirit, and only by the power of his Spirit can people worship him as he really is."

²⁵The woman said to him, "I know that the Messiah will come, and when he comes, he will tell us everything."

²⁶Jesus answered, "I am he, I who am talking with you."

²⁷At that moment Jesus' disciples returned, and they were greatly surprised to find him talking with a woman. But none of them said to her, "What do you want?" or asked him, "Why are you talking with her?"

²⁸Then the woman left her water jar, went back to the town, and said to the people there, ²⁹"Come and see the man who told me everything I have ever done. Could he be the Messiah?" ³⁰So they left the town and went to Jesus.

³¹In the meantime the disciples were begging Jesus, "Teacher, have something to eat!"

³²But he answered, "I have food to eat that you know nothing about."

³³So the disciples started asking among themselves, "Could somebody have brought him food?"

³⁴"My food," Jesus said to them, "is to obey the will of the one who sent me and to finish the work he gave me to do. ³⁵You have a saying, 'Four more months and then the harvest.' But I tell you, take a good look at the fields; the crops are now ripe and ready to be harvested! ³⁶The one who reaps the harvest is being paid and gathers the crops for eternal life; so the one who plants and the one who reaps will be glad together. ³⁷For the saying is true, 'Someone plants, someone else reaps.' ³⁸I have sent you to reap a harvest in a field where you did not work; others worked there, and you profit from their work."

³⁹Many of the Samaritans in that town believed in Jesus because the woman had said, "He told me everything I have ever done." ⁴⁰So when the Samaritans came to him, they begged him to stay with them, and Jesus stayed there two days.

⁴¹Many more believed because of his message, ⁴²and they told the woman, "We believe now, not because of what you said, but because we ourselves

have heard him, and we know that he really is the Savior of the world."

Jesus Heals an Official's Son

⁴³After spending two days there, Jesus left and went to Galilee. ⁴⁴For he himself had said, "Prophets are not respected in their own country." ⁴⁵When he arrived in Galilee, the people there welcomed him, because they had gone to the Passover Festival in Jerusalem and had seen everything that he had done during the festival.

⁴⁶Then Jesus went back to Cana in Galilee, where he had turned the water into wine. A government official was there whose son was sick in Capernaum. ⁴⁷When he heard that Jesus had come from Judea to Galilee, he went to him and asked him to go to Capernaum and heal his son, who was about to die. ⁴⁸Jesus said to him, "None of you will ever believe unless you see miracles and wonders."

⁴⁹"Sir," replied the official, "come with me before my child dies."

⁵⁰Jesus said to him, "Go; your son will live!"

The man believed Jesus' words and went. ⁵¹On his way home his servants met him with the news, "Your boy is going to live!"

⁵²He asked them what time it was when his son got better, and they answered, "It was one o'clock yesterday afternoon when the fever left him." ⁵³Then the father remembered that it was at that very hour when Jesus had told him, "Your son will live." So he and all his family believed.

⁵⁴This was the second miracle that Jesus performed after coming from Judea to Galilee.

The Healing at the Pool

5 After this, Jesus went to Jerusalem for a religious festival. ²Near the Sheep Gate in Jerusalem there is a pool ʰ with five porches; in Hebrew it is called Bethzatha.ⁱ ³A large crowd of sick people were lying on the porches — the blind, the lame, and the paralyzed.ʲ ⁵A man was there who had been sick for thirty-eight years. ⁶Jesus saw him lying there, and he knew that the man had been sick for such a long time; so he asked him, "Do you want to get well?"

⁷The sick man answered, "Sir, I don't have anyone here to put me in the pool when the water is stirred up; while I am trying to get in, somebody else gets there first."

⁸Jesus said to him, "Get up, pick up your mat, and walk." ⁹Immediately the man got well; he picked up his mat and started walking.

The day this happened was a Sabbath, ¹⁰so the Jewish authorities told the man who had been healed, "This is a Sabbath, and it is against our Law for you to carry your mat."

¹¹He answered, "The man who made me well told me to pick up my mat and walk."

¹²They asked him, "Who is the man who told you to do this?"

¹³But the man who had been healed did not know who Jesus was, for there was a crowd in that place, and Jesus had slipped away.

¹⁴Afterward, Jesus found him in the Temple and said, "Listen, you are well now; so stop sinning or something worse may happen to you."

¹⁵Then the man left and told the Jewish authorities that it was Jesus

---

ʰ Near the Sheep Gate . . . a pool; *or* Near the Sheep Pool . . . a place.   ⁱ Bethzatha; *some manuscripts have* Bethesda.   ʲ *Some manuscripts add verses 3b-4:* They were waiting for the water to move, ⁴because every now and then an angel of the Lord went down into the pool and stirred up the water. The first sick person to go into the pool after the water was stirred up was healed from whatever disease he had.
4.44 Mt 13.57; Mk 6.4; Lk 4.24   **4.45** Jn 2.23   **4.46** Jn 2.1-11   **5.10** Ne 13.19; Jr 17.21

who had healed him. 16 So they began to persecute Jesus, because he had done this healing on a Sabbath. 17 Jesus answered them, "My Father is always working, and I too must work."

18 This saying made the Jewish authorities all the more determined to kill him; not only had he broken the Sabbath law, but he had said that God was his own Father and in this way had made himself equal with God.

The Authority of the Son

19 So Jesus answered them, "I tell you the truth: the Son can do nothing on his own; he does only what he sees his Father doing. What the Father does, the Son also does. 20 For the Father loves the Son and shows him all that he himself is doing. He will show him even greater things to do than this, and you will all be amazed. 21 Just as the Father raises the dead and gives them life, in the same way the Son gives life to those he wants to. 22 Nor does the Father himself judge anyone. He has given his Son the full right to judge, 23 so that all will honor the Son in the same way as they honor the Father. Whoever does not honor the Son does not honor the Father who sent him.

24 "I am telling you the truth: those who hear my words and believe in him who sent me have eternal life. They will not be judged, but have already passed from death to life. 25 I am telling you the truth: the time is coming—the time has already come—when the dead will hear the voice of the Son of God, and those who hear it will come to life. 26 Just as the Father is himself the source of life, in the same way he has made his Son to be the source of life. 27 And he has given the Son the right to judge, because he is the Son of Man. 28 Do not be surprised at this; the time is coming when all the dead will hear

his voice 29 and come out of their graves: those who have done good will rise and live, and those who have done evil will rise and be condemned.

Witnesses to Jesus

30 "I can do nothing on my own authority; I judge only as God tells me, so my judgment is right, because I am not trying to do what I want, but only what he who sent me wants.

31 "If I testify on my own behalf, what I say is not to be accepted as real proof. 32 But there is someone else who testifies on my behalf, and I know that what he says about me is true. 33 John is the one to whom you sent your messengers, and he spoke on behalf of the truth. 34 It is not that I must have a human witness; I say this only in order that you may be saved. 35 John was like a lamp, burning and shining, and you were willing for a while to enjoy his light. 36 But I have a witness on my behalf which is even greater than the witness that John gave: what I do, that is, the deeds my Father gave me to do, these speak on my behalf and show that the Father has sent me. 37 And the Father, who sent me, also testifies on my behalf. You have never heard his voice or seen his face, 38 and you do not keep his message in your hearts, for you do not believe in the one whom he sent. 39 You study the Scriptures, because you think that in them you will find eternal life. And these very Scriptures speak about me! 40 Yet you are not willing to come to me in order to have life.

41 "I am not looking for human praise. 42 But I know what kind of people you are, and I know that you have no love for God in your hearts. 43 I have come with my Father's authority, but you have not received me; when, however, someone comes with his own authority,

5.29 Dn 12.2   **5.33** Jn 1.19-27; 3.27-30   **5.37** Mt 3.17; Mk 1.11; Lk 3.22

you will receive him. 44 You like to receive praise from one another, but you do not try to win praise from the one who alone is God; how, then, can you believe me? 45 Do not think, however, that I am the one who will accuse you to my Father. Moses, in whom you have put your hope, is the very one who will accuse you. 46 If you had really believed Moses, you would have believed me, because he wrote about me. 47 But since you do not believe what he wrote, how can you believe what I say?"

Jesus Feeds Five Thousand
(Matthew 14.13-21; Mark 6.30-44;
Luke 9.10-17)

6 After this, Jesus went across Lake Galilee (or, Lake Tiberias, as it is also called). 2 A large crowd followed him, because they had seen his miracles of healing the sick. 3 Jesus went up a hill and sat down with his disciples. 4 The time for the Passover Festival was near. 5 Jesus looked around and saw that a large crowd was coming to him, so he asked Philip, "Where can we buy enough food to feed all these people?" (6 He said this to test Philip; actually he already knew what he would do.)

7 Philip answered, "For everyone to have even a little, it would take more than two hundred silver coins *k* to buy enough bread."

8 Another one of his disciples, Andrew, who was Simon Peter's brother, said, 9 "There is a boy here who has five loaves of barley bread and two fish. But they will certainly not be enough for all these people."

10 "Make the people sit down," Jesus told them. (There was a lot of grass there.) So all the people sat down; there were about five thousand men. 11 Jesus took the bread, gave thanks to God, and distributed it to the people who were sitting there. He did the same with the fish, and they all had as much as they wanted. 12 When they were all full, he said to his disciples, "Gather the pieces left over; let us not waste a bit." 13 So they gathered them all and filled twelve baskets with the pieces left over from the five barley loaves which the people had eaten.

14 Seeing this miracle that Jesus had performed, the people there said, "Surely this is the Prophet *l* who was to come into the world!" 15 Jesus knew that they were about to come and seize him in order to make him king by force; so he went off again to the hills by himself.

Jesus Walks on the Water
(Matthew 14.22-33; Mark 6.45-52)

16 When evening came, Jesus' disciples went down to the lake, 17 got into a boat, and went back across the lake toward Capernaum. Night came on, and Jesus still had not come to them. 18 By then a strong wind was blowing and stirring up the water. 19 The disciples had rowed about three or four miles when they saw Jesus walking on the water, coming near the boat, and they were terrified. 20 "Don't be afraid," Jesus told them, "it is I!" 21 Then they willingly took him into the boat, and immediately the boat reached land at the place they were heading for.

The People Seek Jesus

22 Next day the crowd which had stayed on the other side of the lake realized that there had been only one boat there. They knew that Jesus had not gone in it with his disciples, but that they had left without him. 23 Other boats, which were from Tiberias, came to shore near the place where the crowd had eaten the bread after the Lord had given thanks. 24 When the crowd saw that Jesus was not there, nor his

---

k SILVER COINS: *A silver coin was the daily wage of a rural worker (see Mt 20.2).*
l THE PROPHET: *See 1.21.*

disciples, they got into those boats and went to Capernaum, looking for him.

Jesus the Bread of Life

25 When the people found Jesus on the other side of the lake, they said to him, "Teacher, when did you get here?" **26** Jesus answered, "I am telling you the truth: you are looking for me because you ate the bread and had all you wanted, not because you understood my miracles. **27** Do not work for food that spoils; instead, work for the food that lasts for eternal life. This is the food which the Son of Man will give you, because God, the Father, has put his mark of approval on him."

28 So they asked him, "What can we do in order to do what God wants us to do?"

29 Jesus answered, "What God wants you to do is to believe in the one he sent."

30 They replied, "What miracle will you perform so that we may see it and believe you? What will you do? **31** Our ancestors ate manna in the desert, just as the scripture says, 'He gave them bread from heaven to eat.' "

32 "I am telling you the truth," Jesus said. "What Moses gave you was not*m* the bread from heaven; it is my Father who gives you the real bread from heaven. **33** For the bread that God gives is he who comes down from heaven and gives life to the world."

34 "Sir," they asked him, "give us this bread always."

35 "I am the bread of life," Jesus told them. "Those who come to me will never be hungry; those who believe in me will never be thirsty. **36** Now, I told you that you have seen me but will not believe. **37** Everyone whom my Father gives me will come to me. I will never turn away anyone who comes to me, **38** because I have come down from

heaven to do not my own will but the will of him who sent me. **39** And it is the will of him who sent me that I should not lose any of all those he has given me, but that I should raise them all to life on the last day. **40** For what my Father wants is that all who see the Son and believe in him should have eternal life. And I will raise them to life on the last day."

41 The people started grumbling about him, because he said, "I am the bread that came down from heaven." **42** So they said, "This man is Jesus son of Joseph, isn't he? We know his father and mother. How, then, does he now say he came down from heaven?"

43 Jesus answered, "Stop grumbling among yourselves. **44** People cannot come to me unless the Father who sent me draws them to me; and I will raise them to life on the last day. **45** The prophets wrote, 'Everyone will be taught by God.' Anyone who hears the Father and learns from him comes to me. **46** This does not mean that anyone has seen the Father; he who is from God is the only one who has seen the Father. **47** I am telling you the truth: he who believes has eternal life. **48** I am the bread of life. **49** Your ancestors ate manna in the desert, but they died. **50** But the bread that comes down from heaven is of such a kind that whoever eats it will not die. **51** I am the living bread that came down from heaven. If you eat this bread, you will live forever. The bread that I will give you is my flesh, which I give so that the world may live."

52 This started an angry argument among them. "How can this man give us his flesh to eat?" they asked.

53 Jesus said to them, "I am telling you the truth: if you do not eat the flesh of the Son of Man and drink his blood, you will not have life in yourselves. **54** Those who eat my flesh and drink my

---

m What Moses gave you was not; *or* It was not Moses who gave you.
6.31 Ex 16.4, 15; Ps 78.24   **6.45** Is 54.13

blood have eternal life, and I will raise them to life on the last day. ⁵⁵ For my flesh is the real food; my blood is the real drink. ⁵⁶ Those who eat my flesh and drink my blood live in me, and I live in them. ⁵⁷ The living Father sent me, and because of him I live also. In the same way whoever eats me will live because of me. ⁵⁸ This, then, is the bread that came down from heaven; it is not like the bread that your ancestors ate, but then later died. Those who eat this bread will live forever."

⁵⁹ Jesus said this as he taught in the synagogue in Capernaum.

The Words of Eternal Life

⁶⁰ Many of his followers heard this and said, "This teaching is too hard. Who can listen to it?"

⁶¹ Without being told, Jesus knew that they were grumbling about this, so he said to them, "Does this make you want to give up? ⁶² Suppose, then, that you should see the Son of Man go back up to the place where he was before? ⁶³ What gives life is God's Spirit; human power is of no use at all. The words I have spoken to you bring God's life-giving Spirit. ⁶⁴ Yet some of you do not believe." (Jesus knew from the very beginning who were the ones that would not believe and which one would betray him.) ⁶⁵ And he added, "This is the very reason I told you that no people can come to me unless the Father makes it possible for them to do so."

⁶⁶ Because of this, many of Jesus' followers turned back and would not go with him any more. ⁶⁷ So he asked the twelve disciples, "And you — would you also like to leave?"

⁶⁸ Simon Peter answered him, "Lord, to whom would we go? You have the words that give eternal life. ⁶⁹ And now we believe and know that you are the Holy One who has come from God."

⁷⁰ Jesus replied, "I chose the twelve of you, didn't I? Yet one of you is a devil!"ⁿ ⁷¹ He was talking about Judas, the son of Simon Iscariot. For Judas, even though he was one of the twelve disciples, was going to betray him.

Jesus and His Brothers

7 After this, Jesus traveled in Galilee; he did not want to travel in Judea, because the Jewish authorities there were wanting to kill him. ² The time for the Festival of Shelters was near, ³ so Jesus' brothers said to him, "Leave this place and go to Judea, so that your followers will see the things that you are doing. ⁴ People don't hide what they are doing if they want to be well known. Since you are doing these things, let the whole world know about you!" (⁵ Not even his brothers believed in him.)

⁶ Jesus said to them, "The right time for me has not yet come. Any time is right for you. ⁷ The world cannot hate you, but it hates me, because I keep telling it that its ways are bad. ⁸ You go on to the festival. I am not goingⁿ to this festival, because the right time has not come for me." ⁹ He said this and then stayed on in Galilee.

Jesus at the Festival of Shelters

¹⁰ After his brothers had gone to the festival, Jesus also went; however, he did not go openly, but secretly. ¹¹ The Jewish authorities were looking for him at the festival. "Where is he?" they asked.

¹² There was much whispering about him in the crowd. "He is a good man," some people said. "No," others said, "he fools the people." ¹³ But no one talked about him openly, because they were afraid of the Jewish authorities.

¹⁴ The festival was nearly half over when Jesus went to the Temple and

ⁿ I am not going; *some manuscripts have* I am not yet going.
6.68, 69 Mt 16.16; Mk 8.29; Lk 9.20　　**7.2** Lv 23.34; Dt 16.13

began teaching. [15] The Jewish authorities were greatly surprised and said, "How does this man know so much when he has never been to school?"

[16] Jesus answered, "What I teach is not my own teaching, but it comes from God, who sent me. [17] Whoever is willing to do what God wants will know whether what I teach comes from God or whether I speak on my own authority. [18] Those who speak on their own authority are trying to gain glory for themselves. But he who wants glory for the one who sent him is honest, and there is nothing false in him. [19] Moses gave you the Law, didn't he? But not one of you obeys the Law. Why are you trying to kill me?"

[20] "You have a demon in you!" the crowd answered. "Who is trying to kill you?"

[21] Jesus answered, "I performed one miracle, and you were all surprised. [22] Moses ordered you to circumcise your sons (although it was not Moses but your ancestors who started it), and so you circumcise a boy on the Sabbath. [23] If a boy is circumcised on the Sabbath so that Moses' Law is not broken, why are you angry with me because I made a man completely well on the Sabbath? [24] Stop judging by external standards, and judge by true standards."

Is He the Messiah?

[25] Some of the people of Jerusalem said, "Isn't this the man the authorities are trying to kill? [26] Look! He is talking in public, and they say nothing against him! Can it be that they really know that he is the Messiah? [27] But when the Messiah comes, no one will know where he is from. And we all know where this man comes from."

[28] As Jesus taught in the Temple, he said in a loud voice, "Do you really know me and know where I am from? I have not come on my own authority. He who sent me, however, is truthful. You do not know him, [29] but I know him, because I come from him and he sent me."

[30] Then they tried to seize him, but no one laid a hand on him, because his hour had not yet come. [31] But many in the crowd believed in him and said, "When the Messiah comes, will he perform more miracles than this man has?"

Guards Are Sent to Arrest Jesus

[32] The Pharisees heard the crowd whispering these things about Jesus, so they and the chief priests sent some guards to arrest him. [33] Jesus said, "I shall be with you a little while longer, and then I shall go away to him who sent me. [34] You will look for me, but you will not find me, because you cannot go where I will be."

[35] The Jewish authorities said among themselves, "Where is he about to go so that we shall not find him? Will he go to the Greek cities where our people live, and teach the Greeks? [36] He says that we will look for him but will not find him, and that we cannot go where he will be. What does he mean?"

Streams of Life-Giving Water

[37] On the last and most important day of the festival Jesus stood up and said in a loud voice, "Whoever is thirsty should come to me, and [38] whoever believes in me should drink. As the scripture says, 'Streams of life-giving water will pour out from his side.' "[o] [39] Jesus said this about the Spirit, which those who believed in him were going to receive. At

---

[o] *Jesus' words in verses 37-38 may be translated:* "Whoever is thirsty should come to me and drink. [38] As the scripture says, 'Streams of life-giving water will pour out from within anyone who believes in me.' "

7.22 a Lv 12.3; **b** Gn 17.10   **7.23** Jn 5.9   **7.37** Lv 23.36   **7.38** Ez 47.1; Zec 14.8

that time the Spirit had not yet been given, because Jesus had not been raised to glory.

Division among the People

40Some of the people in the crowd heard him say this and said, "This man is really the Prophet!"*p*

41Others said, "He is the Messiah!"

But others said, "The Messiah will not come from Galilee! **42**The scripture says that the Messiah will be a descendant of King David and will be born in Bethlehem, the town where David lived." **43**So there was a division in the crowd because of Jesus. **44**Some wanted to seize him, but no one laid a hand on him.

The Unbelief of the Jewish Authorities

45When the guards went back, the chief priests and Pharisees asked them, "Why did you not bring him?"

46The guards answered, "Nobody has ever talked the way this man does!"

47"Did he fool you, too?" the Pharisees asked them. **48**"Have you ever known one of the authorities or one Pharisee to believe in him? **49**This crowd does not know the Law of Moses, so they are under God's curse!"

50One of the Pharisees there was Nicodemus, the man who had gone to see Jesus before. He said to the others, **51**"According to our Law we cannot condemn people before hearing them and finding out what they have done."

52"Well," they answered, "are you also from Galilee? Study the Scriptures and you will learn that no prophet ever comes*q* from Galilee."

The Woman Caught in Adultery

8 [Then everyone went home, but Jesus went to the Mount of Olives. **2**Early the next morning he went back to the Temple. All the people gathered around him, and he sat down and began to teach them. **3**The teachers of the Law and the Pharisees brought in a woman who had been caught committing adultery, and they made her stand before them all. **4**"Teacher," they said to Jesus, "this woman was caught in the very act of committing adultery. **5**In our Law Moses commanded that such a woman must be stoned to death. Now, what do you say?" **6**They said this to trap Jesus, so that they could accuse him. But he bent over and wrote on the ground with his finger. **7**As they stood there asking him questions, he straightened up and said to them, "Whichever one of you has committed no sin may throw the first stone at her." **8**Then he bent over again and wrote on the ground. **9**When they heard this, they all left, one by one, the older ones first. Jesus was left alone, with the woman still standing there. **10**He straightened up and said to her, "Where are they? Is there no one left to condemn you?"

11"No one, sir," she answered.

"Well, then," Jesus said, "I do not condemn you either. Go, but do not sin again."]*r*

Jesus the Light of the World

12Jesus spoke to the Pharisees again. "I am the light of the world," he said. "Whoever follows me will have the light of life and will never walk in darkness." **13**The Pharisees said to him, "Now

---

p THE PROPHET: *See 1.21.*   *q* no prophet ever comes; *one manuscript has* the Prophet will not come.   *r Many manuscripts and early translations do not have this passage (8.1-11); others have it after Jn 21.24; others have it after Lk 21.38; one manuscript has it after Jn 7.36.*

7.42 2 S 7.12; Mic 5.2   **7.50** Jn 3.1, 2   **8.5** Lv 20.10; Dt 22.22-24   **8.12** Mt 5.14; Jn 9.5   **8.13** Jn 5.31

you are testifying on your own behalf; what you say proves nothing."

¹⁴"No," Jesus answered, "even though I do testify on my own behalf, what I say is true, because I know where I came from and where I am going. You do not know where I came from or where I am going. ¹⁵You make judgments in a purely human way; I pass judgment on no one. ¹⁶But if I were to do so, my judgment would be true, because I am not alone in this; the Father who sent me is with me. ¹⁷It is written in your Law that when two witnesses agree, what they say is true. ¹⁸I testify on my own behalf, and the Father who sent me also testifies on my behalf."

¹⁹"Where is your father?" they asked him.

"You know neither me nor my Father," Jesus answered. "If you knew me, you would know my Father also."

²⁰Jesus said all this as he taught in the Temple, in the room where the offering boxes were placed. And no one arrested him, because his hour had not come.

You Cannot Go Where I Am Going

²¹Again Jesus said to them, "I will go away; you will look for me, but you will die in your sins. You cannot go where I am going."

²²So the Jewish authorities said, "He says that we cannot go where he is going. Does this mean that he will kill himself?"

²³Jesus answered, "You belong to this world here below, but I come from above. You are from this world, but I am not from this world. ²⁴That is why I told you that you will die in your sins. And you will die in your sins if you do not believe that 'I Am Who I Am'."

²⁵"Who are you?" they asked him.

Jesus answered, "What I have told you from the very beginning.ˢ ²⁶I have much to say about you, much to condemn you for. The one who sent me, however, is truthful, and I tell the world only what I have heard from him."

²⁷They did not understand that Jesus was talking to them about the Father. ²⁸So he said to them, "When you lift up the Son of Man, you will know that 'I Am Who I Am'; then you will know that I do nothing on my own authority, but I say only what the Father has instructed me to say. ²⁹And he who sent me is with me; he has not left me alone, because I always do what pleases him."

³⁰Many who heard Jesus say these things believed in him.

The Truth Will Set You Free

³¹So Jesus said to those who believed in him, "If you obey my teaching, you are really my disciples; ³²you will know the truth, and the truth will set you free."

³³"We are the descendants of Abraham," they answered, "and we have never been anybody's slaves. What do you mean, then, by saying, 'You will be free'?"

³⁴Jesus said to them, "I am telling you the truth: everyone who sins is a slave of sin. ³⁵A slave does not belong to a family permanently, but a son belongs there forever. ³⁶If the Son sets you free, then you will be really free. ³⁷I know you are Abraham's descendants. Yet you are trying to kill me, because you will not accept my teaching. ³⁸I talk about what my Father has shown me, but you do what your father has told you."

³⁹They answered him, "Our father is Abraham."

"If you really were Abraham's children," Jesus replied, "you would doᵗ

ˢ What I have told you from the very beginning; *or* Why should I speak to you at all?

ᵗ If you really were . . . you would do; *some manuscripts have* If you are . . . do.

8.17 Dt 19.15   **8.33** Mt 3.9; Lk 3.8

the same things that he did. 40 All I have ever done is to tell you the truth I heard from God, yet you are trying to kill me. Abraham did nothing like this! 41 You are doing what your father did."

"God himself is the only Father we have," they answered, "and we are his true children."

42 Jesus said to them, "If God really were your Father, you would love me, because I came from God and now I am here. I did not come on my own authority, but he sent me. 43 Why do you not understand what I say? It is because you cannot bear to listen to my message. 44 You are the children of your father, the Devil, and you want to follow your father's desires. From the very beginning he was a murderer and has never been on the side of truth, because there is no truth in him. When he tells a lie, he is only doing what is natural to him, because he is a liar and the father of all lies. 45 But I tell the truth, and that is why you do not believe me. 46 Which one of you can prove that I am guilty of sin? If I tell the truth, then why do you not believe me? 47 He who comes from God listens to God's words. You, however, are not from God, and that is why you will not listen."

Jesus and Abraham

48 They asked Jesus, "Were we not right in saying that you are a Samaritan and have a demon in you?"

49 "I have no demon," Jesus answered. "I honor my Father, but you dishonor me. 50 I am not seeking honor for myself. But there is one who is seeking it and who judges in my favor. 51 I am telling you the truth: whoever obeys my teaching will never die."

52 They said to him, "Now we know for sure that you have a demon! Abraham died, and the prophets died, yet you say that whoever obeys your teach-

ing will never die. 53 Our father Abraham died; you do not claim to be greater than Abraham, do you? And the prophets also died. Who do you think you are?"

54 Jesus answered, "If I were to honor myself, that honor would be worth nothing. The one who honors me is my Father — the very one you say is your God. 55 You have never known him, but I know him. If I were to say that I do not know him, I would be a liar like you. But I do know him, and I obey his word. 56 Your father Abraham rejoiced that he was to see the time of my coming; he saw it and was glad."

57 They said to him, "You are not even fifty years old — and you have seen Abraham?"*u*

58 "I am telling you the truth," Jesus replied. "Before Abraham was born, 'I Am'."

59 Then they picked up stones to throw at him, but Jesus hid himself and left the Temple.

Jesus Heals a Man Born Blind

9 As Jesus was walking along, he saw a man who had been born blind. 2 His disciples asked him, "Teacher, whose sin caused him to be born blind? Was it his own or his parents' sin?"

3 Jesus answered, "His blindness has nothing to do with his sins or his parents' sins. He is blind so that God's power might be seen at work in him. 4 As long as it is day, we must do the work of him who sent me; night is coming when no one can work. 5 While I am in the world, I am the light for the world."

6 After he said this, Jesus spat on the ground and made some mud with the spittle; he rubbed the mud on the man's eyes 7 and told him, "Go and wash your face in the Pool of Siloam."

---

u you have seen Abraham?; *some manuscripts have* has Abraham seen you?
9.5 Mt 5.14; Jn 8.12

(This name means "Sent.") So the man went, washed his face, and came back seeing.

⁸His neighbors, then, and the people who had seen him begging before this, asked, "Isn't this the man who used to sit and beg?"

⁹Some said, "He is the one," but others said, "No he isn't; he just looks like him."

So the man himself said, "I am the man."

¹⁰"How is it that you can now see?" they asked him.

¹¹He answered, "The man called Jesus made some mud, rubbed it on my eyes, and told me to go to Siloam and wash my face. So I went, and as soon as I washed, I could see."

¹²"Where is he?" they asked.

"I don't know," he answered.

The Pharisees Investigate the Healing

¹³Then they took to the Pharisees the man who had been blind. ¹⁴The day that Jesus made the mud and cured him of his blindness was a Sabbath. ¹⁵The Pharisees, then, asked the man again how he had received his sight. He told them, "He put some mud on my eyes; I washed my face, and now I can see."

¹⁶Some of the Pharisees said, "The man who did this cannot be from God, for he does not obey the Sabbath law."

Others, however, said, "How could a man who is a sinner perform such miracles as these?" And there was a division among them.

¹⁷So the Pharisees asked the man once more, "You say he cured you of your blindness — well, what do you say about him?"

"He is a prophet," the man answered.

¹⁸The Jewish authorities, however, were not willing to believe that he had been blind and could now see, until they called his parents ¹⁹and asked them, "Is this your son? You say that he was born blind; how is it, then, that he can now see?"

²⁰His parents answered, "We know that he is our son, and we know that he was born blind. ²¹But we do not know how it is that he is now able to see, nor do we know who cured him of his blindness. Ask him; he is old enough, and he can answer for himself!" ²²His parents said this because they were afraid of the Jewish authorities, who had already agreed that anyone who said he believed that Jesus was the Messiah would be expelled from the synagogue. ²³That is why his parents said, "He is old enough; ask him!"

²⁴A second time they called back the man who had been born blind, and said to him, "Promise before God that you will tell the truth! We know that this man who cured you is a sinner."

²⁵"I do not know if he is a sinner or not," the man replied. "One thing I do know: I was blind, and now I see."

²⁶"What did he do to you?" they asked. "How did he cure you of your blindness?"

²⁷"I have already told you," he answered, "and you would not listen. Why do you want to hear it again? Maybe you, too, would like to be his disciples?"

²⁸They insulted him and said, "You are that fellow's disciple; but we are Moses' disciples. ²⁹We know that God spoke to Moses; as for that fellow, however, we do not even know where he comes from!"

³⁰The man answered, "What a strange thing that is! You do not know where he comes from, but he cured me of my blindness! ³¹We know that God does not listen to sinners; he does listen to people who respect him and do what he wants them to do. ³²Since the beginning of the world nobody has ever heard of anyone giving sight to a person born blind. ³³Unless this man came from God, he would not be able to do a thing."

³⁴They answered, "You were born and brought up in sin — and you are try-

ing to teach us?" And they expelled him from the synagogue.

Spiritual Blindness

³⁵When Jesus heard what had happened, he found the man and asked him, "Do you believe in the Son of Man?"

³⁶The man answered, "Tell me who he is, sir, so that I can believe in him!"

³⁷Jesus said to him, "You have already seen him, and he is the one who is talking with you now."

³⁸"I believe, Lord!" the man said, and knelt down before Jesus.

³⁹Jesus said, "I came to this world to judge, so that the blind should see and those who see should become blind."

⁴⁰Some Pharisees who were there with him heard him say this and asked him, "Surely you don't mean that we are blind, too?"

⁴¹Jesus answered, "If you were blind, then you would not be guilty; but since you claim that you can see, this means that you are still guilty."

The Parable of the Shepherd

10 Jesus said, "I am telling you the truth: the man who does not enter the sheep pen by the gate, but climbs in some other way, is a thief and a robber. ²The man who goes in through the gate is the shepherd of the sheep. ³The gatekeeper opens the gate for him; the sheep hear his voice as he calls his own sheep by name, and he leads them out. ⁴When he has brought them out, he goes ahead of them, and the sheep follow him, because they know his voice. ⁵They will not follow someone else; instead, they will run away from such a person, because they do not know his voice."

⁶Jesus told them this parable, but they did not understand what he meant.

Jesus the Good Shepherd

⁷So Jesus said again, "I am telling you the truth: I am the gate for the sheep. ⁸All others who came before me are thieves and robbers, but the sheep did not listen to them. ⁹I am the gate. Those who come in by me will be saved; they will come in and go out and find pasture. ¹⁰The thief comes only in order to steal, kill, and destroy. I have come in order that you might have life — life in all its fullness.

¹¹"I am the good shepherd, who is willing to die for the sheep. ¹²When the hired man, who is not a shepherd and does not own the sheep, sees a wolf coming, he leaves the sheep and runs away; so the wolf snatches the sheep and scatters them. ¹³The hired man runs away because he is only a hired man and does not care about the sheep. ¹⁴⁻¹⁵I am the good shepherd. As the Father knows me and I know the Father, in the same way I know my sheep and they know me. And I am willing to die for them. ¹⁶There are other sheep which belong to me that are not in this sheep pen. I must bring them, too; they will listen to my voice, and they will become^v one flock with one shepherd.

¹⁷"The Father loves me because I am willing to give up my life, in order that I may receive it back again. ¹⁸No one takes my life away from me. I give it up of my own free will. I have the right to give it up, and I have the right to take it back. This is what my Father has commanded me to do."

¹⁹Again there was a division among the people because of these words. ²⁰Many of them were saying, "He has a demon! He is crazy! Why do you listen to him?"

²¹But others were saying, "A man with a demon could not talk like this!

---

^v they will become; *some manuscripts have* there will be.
10.15 Mt 11.27; Lk 10.22

How could a demon give sight to blind people?"

Jesus Is Rejected

22 It was winter, and the Festival of the Dedication of the Temple was being celebrated in Jerusalem. 23 Jesus was walking in Solomon's Porch in the Temple, 24 when the people gathered around him and asked, "How long are you going to keep us in suspense? Tell us the plain truth: are you the Messiah?"

25 Jesus answered, "I have already told you, but you would not believe me. The deeds I do by my Father's authority speak on my behalf; 26 but you will not believe, for you are not my sheep. 27 My sheep listen to my voice; I know them, and they follow me. 28 I give them eternal life, and they shall never die. No one can snatch them away from me. 29 What my Father has given me is greater*w* than everything, and no one can snatch them away from the Father's care. 30 The Father and I are one."

31 Then the people again picked up stones to throw at him. 32 Jesus said to them, "I have done many good deeds in your presence which the Father gave me to do; for which one of these do you want to stone me?"

33 They answered, "We do not want to stone you because of any good deeds, but because of your blasphemy! You are only a man, but you are trying to make yourself God!"

34 Jesus answered, "It is written in your own Law that God said, 'You are gods.' 35 We know that what the scripture says is true forever; and God called those people gods, the people to whom his message was given. 36 As for me, the Father chose me and sent me into the world. How, then, can you say that I blaspheme because I said that I am the Son of God? 37 Do not believe me, then, if I am not doing the things my Father wants me to do. 38 But if I do them, even though you do not believe me, you should at least believe my deeds, in order that you may know once and for all that the Father is in me and that I am in the Father."

39 Once more they tried to seize Jesus, but he slipped out of their hands.

40 Jesus then went back again across the Jordan River to the place where John had been baptizing, and he stayed there. 41 Many people came to him. "John performed no miracles," they said, "but everything he said about this man was true." 42 And many people there believed in him.

The Death of Lazarus

11 A man named Lazarus, who lived in Bethany, became sick. Bethany was the town where Mary and her sister Martha lived. (2 This Mary was the one who poured the perfume on the Lord's feet and wiped them with her hair; it was her brother Lazarus who was sick.) 3 The sisters sent Jesus a message: "Lord, your dear friend is sick."

4 When Jesus heard it, he said, "The final result of this sickness will not be the death of Lazarus; this has happened in order to bring glory to God, and it will be the means by which the Son of God will receive glory."

5 Jesus loved Martha and her sister and Lazarus. 6 Yet when he received the news that Lazarus was sick, he stayed where he was for two more days. 7 Then he said to the disciples, "Let us go back to Judea."

8 "Teacher," the disciples answered,

---

w What my Father has given me is greater; *some manuscripts have* My Father, who gave them to me, is greater.
10.33 Lv 24.16   **10.34** Ps 82.6   **10.40** Jn 1.28   **11.1** Lk 10.38, 39   **11.2** Jn 12.3

"just a short time ago the people there wanted to stone you; and are you planning to go back?"

⁹Jesus said, "A day has twelve hours, doesn't it? So those who walk in broad daylight do not stumble, for they see the light of this world. ¹⁰But if they walk during the night they stumble, because they have no light." ¹¹Jesus said this and then added, "Our friend Lazarus has fallen asleep, but I will go and wake him up."

¹²The disciples answered, "If he is asleep, Lord, he will get well."

¹³Jesus meant that Lazarus had died, but they thought he meant natural sleep. ¹⁴So Jesus told them plainly, "Lazarus is dead, ¹⁵but for your sake I am glad that I was not with him, so that you will believe. Let us go to him."

¹⁶Thomas (called the Twin) said to his fellow disciples, "Let us all go along with the Teacher, so that we may die with him!"

Jesus the Resurrection and the Life

¹⁷When Jesus arrived, he found that Lazarus had been buried four days before. ¹⁸Bethany was less than two miles from Jerusalem, ¹⁹and many Judeans had come to see Martha and Mary to comfort them about their brother's death.

²⁰When Martha heard that Jesus was coming, she went out to meet him, but Mary stayed in the house. ²¹Martha said to Jesus, "If you had been here, Lord, my brother would not have died! ²²But I know that even now God will give you whatever you ask him for."

²³"Your brother will rise to life," Jesus told her.

²⁴"I know," she replied, "that he will rise to life on the last day."

²⁵Jesus said to her, "I am the resurrection and the life. Those who believe in me will live, even though they die; ²⁶and those who live and believe in me will never die. Do you believe this?"

²⁷"Yes, Lord!" she answered. "I do believe that you are the Messiah, the Son of God, who was to come into the world."

Jesus Weeps

²⁸After Martha said this, she went back and called her sister Mary privately. "The Teacher is here," she told her, "and is asking for you." ²⁹When Mary heard this, she got up and hurried out to meet him. (³⁰Jesus had not yet arrived in the village, but was still in the place where Martha had met him.) ³¹The people who were in the house with Mary comforting her followed her when they saw her get up and hurry out. They thought that she was going to the grave to weep there.

³²Mary arrived where Jesus was, and as soon as she saw him, she fell at his feet. "Lord," she said, "if you had been here, my brother would not have died!"

³³Jesus saw her weeping, and he saw how the people with her were weeping also; his heart was touched, and he was deeply moved. ³⁴"Where have you buried him?" he asked them.

"Come and see, Lord," they answered.

³⁵Jesus wept. ³⁶"See how much he loved him!" the people said.

³⁷But some of them said, "He gave sight to the blind man, didn't he? Could he not have kept Lazarus from dying?"

Lazarus Is Brought to Life

³⁸Deeply moved once more, Jesus went to the tomb, which was a cave with a stone placed at the entrance. ³⁹"Take the stone away!" Jesus ordered.

Martha, the dead man's sister, answered, "There will be a bad smell, Lord. He has been buried four days!"

⁴⁰Jesus said to her, "Didn't I tell you that you would see God's glory if you

believed?" [41] They took the stone away. Jesus looked up and said, "I thank you, Father, that you listen to me. [42] I know that you always listen to me, but I say this for the sake of the people here, so that they will believe that you sent me." [43] After he had said this, he called out in

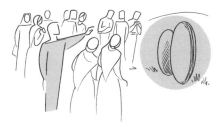

"Lazarus, come out!" (11.43)

a loud voice, "Lazarus, come out!" [44] He came out, his hands and feet wrapped in grave cloths, and with a cloth around his face. "Untie him," Jesus told them, "and let him go."

The Plot against Jesus
(Matthew 26.1-5; Mark 14.1, 2;
Luke 22.1, 2)

[45] Many of the people who had come to visit Mary saw what Jesus did, and they believed in him. [46] But some of them returned to the Pharisees and told them what Jesus had done. [47] So the Pharisees and the chief priests met with the Council and said, "What shall we do? Look at all the miracles this man is performing! [48] If we let him go on in this way, everyone will believe in him, and the Roman authorities will take action and destroy our Temple and our nation!"

[49] One of them, named Caiaphas, who was High Priest that year, said, "What fools you are! [50] Don't you realize that it is better for you to have one man die for the people, instead of having the whole nation destroyed?" [51] Actually, he did not say this of his own accord; rather, as he was High Priest that year, he was prophesying that Jesus was going to die for the Jewish people, [52] and not only for them, but also to bring together into one body all the scattered people of God.

[53] From that day on the Jewish authorities made plans to kill Jesus. [54] So Jesus did not travel openly in Judea, but left and went to a place near the desert, to a town named Ephraim, where he stayed with the disciples.

[55] The time for the Passover Festival was near, and many people went up from the country to Jerusalem to perform the ritual of purification before the festival. [56] They were looking for Jesus, and as they gathered in the Temple, they asked one another, "What do you think? Surely he will not come to the festival, will he?" [57] The chief priests and the Pharisees had given orders that if anyone knew where Jesus was, he must report it, so that they could arrest him.

Jesus Is Anointed at Bethany
(Matthew 26.6-13; Mark 14.3-9)

12 Six days before the Passover, Jesus went to Bethany, the home of Lazarus, the man he had raised from death. [2] They prepared a dinner for him there, which Martha helped serve; Lazarus was one of those who were sitting at the table with Jesus. [3] Then Mary took a whole pint of a very expensive perfume made of pure nard, poured it on Jesus' feet, and wiped them with her hair. The sweet smell of the perfume filled the whole house. [4] One of Jesus' disciples, Judas Iscariot — the one who was going to betray him — said, [5] "Why wasn't this perfume sold for three hundred silver coins[x] and the money given to the poor?" [6] He said this, not because he

[x] SILVER COINS: *See* 6.7.
12.3 Lk 7.37, 38

cared about the poor, but because he was a thief. He carried the money bag and would help himself from it.

7 But Jesus said, "Leave her alone! Let her keep what she has for the day of my burial. 8 You will always have poor people with you, but you will not always have me."

The Plot against Lazarus

9 A large number of people heard that Jesus was in Bethany, so they went there, not only because of Jesus but also to see Lazarus, whom Jesus had raised from death. 10 So the chief priests made plans to kill Lazarus too, 11 because on his account many Jews were rejecting them and believing in Jesus.

The Triumphant Entry into Jerusalem
(Matthew 21.1-11; Mark 11.1-11;
Luke 19.28-40)

12 The next day the large crowd that had come to the Passover Festival heard that Jesus was coming to Jerusalem. 13 So they took branches of palm trees and went out to meet him, shouting, "Praise God! God bless him who comes in the name of the Lord! God bless the King of Israel!"

14 Jesus found a donkey and rode on it, just as the scripture says,

15 "Do not be afraid, city of Zion!
    Here comes your king,
        riding on a young donkey."

16 His disciples did not understand this at the time; but when Jesus had been raised to glory, they remembered that the scripture said this about him and that they had done this for him. 17 The people who had been with Jesus when he called Lazarus out of the grave and raised him from death had reported what had happened. 18 That was why the crowd met him — because they heard that he had performed this miracle. 19 The Pharisees then said to one another, "You see, we are not succeeding at all! Look, the whole world is following him!"

Some Greeks Seek Jesus

20 Some Greeks were among those who had gone to Jerusalem to worship during the festival. 21 They went to Philip (he was from Bethsaida in Galilee) and said, "Sir, we want to see Jesus."

22 Philip went and told Andrew, and the two of them went and told Jesus. 23 Jesus answered them, "The hour has now come for the Son of Man to receive great glory. 24 I am telling you the truth: a grain of wheat remains no more than a single grain unless it is dropped into the ground and dies. If it does die, then it produces many grains. 25 Those who love their own life will lose it; those who hate their own life in this world will keep it for life eternal. 26 Whoever wants to serve me must follow me, so that my servant will be with me where I am. And my Father will honor anyone who serves me.

Jesus Speaks about His Death

27 "Now my heart is troubled — and what shall I say? Shall I say, 'Father, do not let this hour come upon me'? But that is why I came — so that I might go through this hour of suffering. 28 Father, bring glory to your name!"

Then a voice spoke from heaven, "I have brought glory to it, and I will do so again."

29 The crowd standing there heard the voice, and some of them said it was thunder, while others said, "An angel spoke to him!"

30 But Jesus said to them, "It was not for my sake that this voice spoke, but for yours. 31 Now is the time for this world to be judged; now the ruler of this world will be overthrown. 32 When I am

12.8 Dt 15.11 **12.13** Ps 118.25, 26 **12.15** Zec 9.9 **12.25** Mt 10.39; 16.25; Mk 8.35; Lk 9.24; 17.33

lifted up from the earth, I will draw everyone to me." (33 In saying this he indicated the kind of death he was going to suffer.)

34 The crowd answered, "Our Law tells us that the Messiah will live forever. How, then, can you say that the Son of Man must be lifted up? Who is this Son of Man?"

35 Jesus answered, "The light will be among you a little longer. Continue on your way while you have the light, so that the darkness will not come upon you; for the one who walks in the dark does not know where he is going. 36 Believe in the light, then, while you have it, so that you will be the people of the light."

The Unbelief of the People

After Jesus said this, he went off and hid himself from them. 37 Even though he had performed all these miracles in their presence, they did not believe in him, 38 so that what the prophet Isaiah had said might come true:

"Lord, who believed the message
    we told?
To whom did the Lord reveal
    his power?"

39 And so they were not able to believe, because Isaiah also said,

40 "God has blinded their eyes
    and closed their minds,
so that their eyes would not see,
    and their minds would not
        understand,
and they would not turn to
    me, says God,
for me to heal them."

41 Isaiah said this because he saw Jesus' glory and spoke about him.

42 Even then, many Jewish authorities believed in Jesus; but because of the Pharisees they did not talk about it openly, so as not to be expelled from the synagogue. 43 They loved human approval rather than the approval of God.

Judgment by Jesus' Words

44 Jesus said in a loud voice, "Whoever believes in me believes not only in me but also in him who sent me. 45 Whoever sees me sees also him who sent me. 46 I have come into the world as light, so that everyone who believes in me should not remain in the darkness. 47 If people hear my message and do not obey it, I will not judge them. I came, not to judge the world, but to save it. 48 Those who reject me and do not accept my message have one who will judge them. The words I have spoken will be their judge on the last day! 49 This is true, because I have not spoken on my own authority, but the Father who sent me has commanded me what I must say and speak. 50 And I know that his command brings eternal life. What I say, then, is what the Father has told me to say."

Jesus Washes His Disciples' Feet

13 It was now the day before the Passover Festival. Jesus knew that the hour had come for him to leave this world and go to the Father. He had always loved those in the world who were his own, and he loved them to the very end.

2 Jesus and his disciples were at supper. The Devil had already put into the heart of Judas, the son of Simon Iscariot, the thought of betraying Jesus.y 3 Jesus knew that the Father had given him complete power; he knew that he had come from God and was going to God. 4 So he rose from the table, took off his outer garment, and tied a towel around his waist. 5 Then he poured some water into a washbasin and began to wash the disciples' feet and dry them

---

y The Devil . . . betraying Jesus; *or* The Devil had already decided that Judas, the son of Simon Iscariot, would betray Jesus.

12.34 Ps 110.4; Is 9.7; Ez 37.25; Dn 7.14   **12.38** Is 53.1 (LXX)   **12.40** Is 6.10 (LXX)

The disciples looked at one another. (13.22)

with the towel around his waist. ⁶He came to Simon Peter, who said to him, "Are you going to wash my feet, Lord?"

⁷Jesus answered him, "You do not understand now what I am doing, but you will understand later."

⁸Peter declared, "Never at any time will you wash my feet!"

"If I do not wash your feet," Jesus answered, "you will no longer be my disciple."

⁹Simon Peter answered, "Lord, do not wash only my feet, then! Wash my hands and head, too!"

¹⁰Jesus said, "Those who have taken a bath are completely clean and do not have to wash themselves, except for their feet.ᶻ All of you are clean — all except one." (¹¹Jesus already knew who was going to betray him; that is why he said, "All of you, except one, are clean.")

¹²After Jesus had washed their feet, he put his outer garment back on and returned to his place at the table. "Do you understand what I have just done to you?" he asked. ¹³"You call me Teacher and Lord, and it is right that you do so, because that is what I am. ¹⁴I, your Lord and Teacher, have just washed your feet. You, then, should wash one another's feet. ¹⁵I have set an example for you, so that you will do just what I have done for you. ¹⁶I am telling you the truth: no slaves are greater than their master, and no messengers are greater than the one who sent them. ¹⁷Now that you know this truth, how happy you will be if you put it into practice!

¹⁸"I am not talking about all of you; I know those I have chosen. But the scripture must come true that says, 'The man who shared my food turned against me.' ¹⁹I tell you this now before it happens, so that when it does happen, you will believe that 'I Am Who I Am.' ²⁰I am telling you the truth: whoever receives anyone I send receives me also; and whoever receives me receives him who sent me."

Jesus Predicts His Betrayal
(Matthew 26.20-25; Mark 14.17-21; Luke 22.21-23)

²¹After Jesus had said this, he was deeply troubled and declared openly, "I am telling you the truth: one of you is going to betray me."

²²The disciples looked at one another, completely puzzled about whom he meant. ²³One of the disciples, the one whom Jesus loved, was sitting next to Jesus. ²⁴Simon Peter motioned to him and said, "Ask him whom he is talking about."

²⁵So that disciple moved closer to Jesus' side and asked, "Who is it, Lord?"

²⁶Jesus answered, "I will dip some bread in the sauce and give it to him; he is the man." So he took a piece of bread, dipped it, and gave it to Judas, the son of Simon Iscariot. ²⁷As soon as Judas took the bread, Satan entered into him. Jesus said to him, "Hurry and do what you must!" ²⁸None of the others at the table understood why Jesus said this to him. ²⁹Since Judas was in charge of the

---

ᶻ *Some manuscripts do not have* except for their feet.
13.12-15 Lk 22.27   **13.16** Mt 10.24; Lk 6.40; Jn 15.20   **13.18** Ps 41.9   **13.20** Mt 10.40; Mk 9.37; Lk 9.48; 10.16

money bag, some of the disciples thought that Jesus had told him to go and buy what they needed for the festival, or to give something to the poor.

30 Judas accepted the bread and went out at once. It was night.

The New Commandment

31 After Judas had left, Jesus said, "Now the Son of Man's glory is revealed; now God's glory is revealed through him. **32** And if God's glory is revealed through him, then God will reveal the glory of the Son of Man in himself, and he will do so at once. **33** My children, I shall not be with you very much longer. You will look for me; but I tell you now what I told the Jewish authorities, 'You cannot go where I am going.' **34** And now I give you a new commandment: love one another. As I have loved you, so you must love one another. **35** If you have love for one another, then everyone will know that you are my disciples."

Jesus Predicts Peter's Denial
(Matthew 26.31-35; Mark 14.27-31; Luke 22.31-34)

36 "Where are you going, Lord?" Simon Peter asked him.

"You cannot follow me now where I am going," answered Jesus; "but later you will follow me."

37 "Lord, why can't I follow you now?" asked Peter. "I am ready to die for you!"

38 Jesus answered, "Are you really ready to die for me? I am telling you the truth: before the rooster crows you will say three times that you do not know me.

Jesus the Way to the Father

14 "Do not be worried and upset," Jesus told them. "Believe*a* in God and believe also in me. **2** There are many rooms in my Father's house, and I am going to prepare a place for you. I would not tell you this if it were not so.*b* **3** And after I go and prepare a place for you, I will come back and take you to myself, so that you will be where I am. **4** You know the way that leads to the place where I am going."

5 Thomas said to him, "Lord, we do not know where you are going; so how can we know the way to get there?"

6 Jesus answered him, "I am the way, the truth, and the life; no one goes to the Father except by me. **7** Now that you have known me," he said to them, "you will know*c* my Father also, and from now on you do know him and you have seen him."

8 Philip said to him, "Lord, show us the Father; that is all we need."

9 Jesus answered, "For a long time I have been with you all; yet you do not know me, Philip? Whoever has seen me has seen the Father. Why, then, do you say, 'Show us the Father'? **10** Do you not believe, Philip, that I am in the Father and the Father is in me? The words that I have spoken to you," Jesus said to his disciples, "do not come from me. The Father, who remains in me, does his own work. **11** Believe me when I say that I am in the Father and the Father is in me. If not, believe because of the things I do. **12** I am telling you the truth: those who believe in me will do what I do — yes, they will do even greater things, because I am going to the Father. **13** And I will do whatever you ask for in my name, so that the Father's glory will be shown through the Son. **14** If you

---

a Believe; *or* You believe.　　*b* There are . . . were not so; *or* There are many rooms in my Father's house; if it were not so, would I tell you that I am going to prepare a place for you?　　*c* Now that you have known me . . . you will know; *some manuscripts have* If you had known me . . . you would know.

13.33 Jn 7.34　**13.34** Jn 15.12, 17; 1 Jn 3.23; 2 Jn 5

ask me[d] for anything in my name, I will do it.

The Promise of the Holy Spirit

15 "If you love me, you will obey my commandments. [16] I will ask the Father, and he will give you another Helper, who will stay with you forever. [17] He is the Spirit, who reveals the truth about God. The world cannot receive him, because it cannot see him or know him. But you know him, because he remains with you and is[e] in you.

[18] "When I go, you will not be left all alone; I will come back to you. [19] In a little while the world will see me no more, but you will see me; and because I live, you also will live. [20] When that day comes, you will know that I am in my Father and that you are in me, just as I am in you.

[21] "Those who accept my commandments and obey them are the ones who love me. My Father will love those who love me; I too will love them and reveal myself to them."

[22] Judas (not Judas Iscariot) said, "Lord, how can it be that you will reveal yourself to us and not to the world?"

[23] Jesus answered him, "Those who love me will obey my teaching. My Father will love them, and my Father and I will come to them and live with them. [24] Those who do not love me do not obey my teaching. And the teaching you have heard is not mine, but comes from the Father, who sent me.

[25] "I have told you this while I am still with you. [26] The Helper, the Holy Spirit, whom the Father will send in my name, will teach you everything and make you remember all that I have told you.

[27] "Peace is what I leave with you; it is my own peace that I give you. I do not give it as the world does. Do not be worried and upset; do not be afraid. [28] You heard me say to you, 'I am leaving, but I will come back to you.' If you loved me, you would be glad that I am going to the Father; for he is greater than I. [29] I have told you this now before it all happens, so that when it does happen, you will believe. [30] I cannot talk with you much longer, because the ruler of this world is coming. He has no power over me, [31] but the world must know that I love the Father; that is why I do everything as he commands me.

"Come, let us go from this place.

Jesus the Real Vine

15 "I am the real vine, and my Father is the gardener. [2] He breaks off every branch in me that does not bear fruit, and he prunes every branch that does bear fruit, so that it will be clean and bear more fruit. [3] You have been made clean already by the teaching I have given you. [4] Remain united to me, and I will remain united to you. A branch cannot bear fruit by itself; it can do so only if it remains in the vine. In the same way you cannot bear fruit unless you remain in me.

[5] "I am the vine, and you are the branches. Those who remain in me, and I in them, will bear much fruit; for you can do nothing without me. [6] Those who do not remain in me are thrown out like a branch and dry up; such branches are gathered up and thrown into the fire, where they are burned. [7] If you remain in me and my words remain in you, then you will ask for anything you wish, and you shall have it. [8] My Father's glory is shown by your bearing much fruit; and in this way you become my disciples. [9] I love you just as the Father loves me; remain in my love. [10] If you obey my commands, you will remain in my love, just as I have obeyed my Father's commands and remain in his love.

[11] "I have told you this so that my joy

---

[d] *Some manuscripts do not have* me.   [e] is; *some manuscripts have* will be.

may be in you and that your joy may be complete. ¹²My commandment is this: love one another, just as I love you. ¹³The greatest love you can have for your friends is to give your life for them. ¹⁴And you are my friends if you do what I command you. ¹⁵I do not call you servants any longer, because servants do not know what their master is doing. Instead, I call you friends, because I have told you everything I heard from my Father. ¹⁶You did not choose me; I chose you and appointed you to go and bear much fruit, the kind of fruit that endures. And so the Father will give you whatever you ask of him in my name. ¹⁷This, then, is what I command you: love one another.

The World's Hatred

¹⁸"If the world hates you, just remember that it has hated me first. ¹⁹If you belonged to the world, then the world would love you as its own. But I chose you from this world, and you do not belong to it; that is why the world hates you. ²⁰Remember what I told you: 'Slaves are not greater than their master.' If people persecuted me, they will persecute you too; if they obeyed my teaching, they will obey yours too. ²¹But they will do all this to you because you are mine; for they do not know the one who sent me. ²²They would not have been guilty of sin if I had not come and spoken to them; as it is, they no longer have any excuse for their sin. ²³Whoever hates me hates my Father also. ²⁴They would not have been guilty of sin if I had not done among them the things that no one else ever did; as it is, they have seen what I did, and they hate both me and my Father. ²⁵This, however, was bound to happen so that what is written in their Law may come true: 'They hated me for no reason at all.'

²⁶"The Helper will come – the Spirit, who reveals the truth about God and who comes from the Father. I will send him to you from the Father, and he will speak about me. ²⁷And you, too, will speak about me, because you have been with me from the very beginning.

16 "I have told you this, so that you will not give up your faith. ²You will be expelled from the synagogues, and the time will come when those who kill you will think that by doing this they are serving God. ³People will do these things to you because they have not known either the Father or me. ⁴But I have told you this, so that when the time comes for them to do these things, you will remember what I told you.

The Work of the Holy Spirit

"I did not tell you these things at the beginning, for I was with you. ⁵But now I am going to him who sent me, yet none of you asks me where I am going. ⁶And now that I have told you, your hearts are full of sadness. ⁷But I am telling you the truth: it is better for you that I go away, because if I do not go, the Helper will not come to you. But if I do go away, then I will send him to you. ⁸And when he comes, he will prove to the people of the world that they are wrong about sin and about what is right and about God's judgment. ⁹They are wrong about sin, because they do not believe in me; ¹⁰they are wrong about what is right, because I am going to the Father and you will not see me any more; ¹¹and they are wrong about judgment, because the ruler of this world has already been judged.

¹²"I have much more to tell you, but now it would be too much for you to bear. ¹³When, however, the Spirit comes, who reveals the truth about

15.12 Jn 13.34; 15.17; 1 Jn 3.23; 2 Jn 5   **15.20** Mt 10.24; Lk 6.40; Jn 13.16
15.25 Ps 35.19; 69.4

God, he will lead you into all the truth. He will not speak on his own authority, but he will speak of what he hears and will tell you of things to come. 14 He will give me glory, because he will take what I say and tell it to you. 15 All that my Father has is mine; that is why I said that the Spirit will take what I give him and tell it to you.

Sadness and Gladness

16 "In a little while you will not see me any more, and then a little while later you will see me."

17 Some of his disciples asked among themselves, "What does this mean? He tells us that in a little while we will not see him, and then a little while later we will see him; and he also says, 'It is because I am going to the Father.' 18 What does this 'a little while' mean? We don't know what he is talking about!"

19 Jesus knew that they wanted to question him, so he said to them, "I said, 'In a little while you will not see me, and then a little while later you will see me.' Is this what you are asking about among yourselves? 20 I am telling you the truth: you will cry and weep, but the world will be glad; you will be sad, but your sadness will turn into gladness. 21 When a woman is about to give birth, she is sad because her hour of suffering has come; but when the baby is born, she forgets her suffering, because she is happy that a baby has been born into the world. 22 That is how it is with you: now you are sad, but I will see you again, and your hearts will be filled with gladness, the kind of gladness that no one can take away from you.

23 "When that day comes, you will not ask me for anything. I am telling you the truth: the Father will give you whatever you ask of him in my name.f 24 Until now you have not asked for any-

thing in my name; ask and you will receive, so that your happiness may be complete.

Victory over the World

25 "I have used figures of speech to tell you these things. But the time will come when I will not use figures of speech, but will speak to you plainly about the Father. 26 When that day comes, you will ask him in my name; and I do not say that I will ask him on your behalf, 27 for the Father himself loves you. He loves you because you love me and have believed that I came from God. 28 I did come from the Father, and I came into the world; and now I am leaving the world and going to the Father."

29 Then his disciples said to him, "Now you are speaking plainly, without using figures of speech. 30 We know now that you know everything; you do not need to have someone ask you questions. This makes us believe that you came from God."

31 Jesus answered them, "Do you believe now? 32 The time is coming, and is already here, when all of you will be scattered, each of you to your own home, and I will be left all alone. But I am not really alone, because the Father is with me. 33 I have told you this so that you will have peace by being united to me. The world will make you suffer. But be brave! I have defeated the world!"

Jesus Prays for His Disciples

17 After Jesus finished saying this, he looked up to heaven and said, "Father, the hour has come. Give glory to your Son, so that the Son may give glory to you. 2 For you gave him authority over all people, so that he might give eternal life to all those you

---

f the Father will give you whatever you ask of him in my name; *some manuscripts have* if you ask the Father for anything, he will give it to you in my name.

"Father, the hour has come." (17.1)

I came from you, and they believe that you sent me.

9"I pray for them. I do not pray for the world but for those you gave me, for they belong to you. 10 All I have is yours, and all you have is mine; and my glory is shown through them. 11 And now I am coming to you; I am no longer in the world, but they are in the world. Holy Father! Keep them safe by the power of your name, the name you gave me,*g* so that they may be one just as you and I are one. 12 While I was with them, I kept them safe by the power of your name, the name you gave me.*h* I protected them, and not one of them was lost, except the man who was bound to be lost — so that the scripture might come true. 13 And now I am coming to you, and I say these things in the world so that they might have my joy in their hearts in all its fullness. 14 I gave them your message, and the world hated them, because they do not belong to the world, just as I do not belong to the world. 15 I do not ask you to take them out of the world, but I do ask you to keep them safe from the Evil One. 16 Just as I do not belong to the world, they do not belong to the world. 17 Dedicate them to yourself by means of the truth; your word is truth. 18 I sent them into the world, just as you sent me into the world. 19 And for their sake I dedicate myself to you, in order that they, too, may be truly dedicated to you.

20"I pray not only for them, but also for those who believe in me because of their message. 21 I pray that they may all be one. Father! May they be in us, just as you are in me and I am in you. May they be one, so that the world will believe that you sent me. 22 I gave them the same glory you gave me, so that

gave him. 3 And eternal life means to know you, the only true God, and to know Jesus Christ, whom you sent. 4 I have shown your glory on earth; I have finished the work you gave me to do. 5 Father! Give me glory in your presence now, the same glory I had with you before the world was made.

6"I have made you known to those you gave me out of the world. They belonged to you, and you gave them to me. They have obeyed your word, 7 and now they know that everything you gave me comes from you. 8 I gave them the message that you gave me, and they received it; they know that it is true that

---

g Keep them safe by the power of your name, the name you gave me; *some manuscripts have* By the power of your name keep safe those you have given me.
h I kept them safe by the power of your name, the name you gave me; *some manuscripts have* By the power of your name I kept safe those you have given me.
17.12 Ps 41.9; Jn 13.18

they may be one, just as you and I are one: 23 I in them and you in me, so that they may be completely one, in order that the world may know that you sent me and that you love them as you love me.

24"Father! You have given them to me, and I want them to be with me where I am, so that they may see my glory, the glory you gave me; for you loved me before the world was made. 25 Righteous Father! The world does not know you, but I know you, and these know that you sent me. 26 I made you known to them, and I will continue to do so, in order that the love you have for me may be in them, and so that I also may be in them."

The Arrest of Jesus
(Matthew 26.47-56; Mark 14.43-50; Luke 22.47-53)

18 After Jesus had said this prayer, he left with his disciples and went across Kidron Brook. There was a garden in that place, and Jesus and his disciples went in. 2 Judas, the traitor, knew where it was, because many times Jesus had met there with his disciples. 3 So Judas went to the garden, taking with him a group of Roman soldiers, and some Temple guards sent by the chief priests and the Pharisees; they were armed and carried lanterns and torches. 4 Jesus knew everything that was going to happen to him, so he stepped forward and asked them, "Who is it you are looking for?"

5 "Jesus of Nazareth," they answered.

"I am he," he said.

Judas, the traitor, was standing there with them. 6 When Jesus said to them, "I am he," they moved back and fell to the ground. 7 Again Jesus asked them, "Who is it you are looking for?"

"Jesus of Nazareth," they said.

8 "I have already told you that I am he," Jesus said. "If, then, you are looking for me, let these others go." (9 He said this so that what he had said might come true: "Father, I have not lost even one of those you gave me.")

10 Simon Peter, who had a sword, drew it and struck the High Priest's slave, cutting off his right ear. The name of the slave was Malchus. 11 Jesus said to Peter, "Put your sword back in its place! Do you think that I will not drink the cup of suffering which my Father has given me?"

Jesus before Annas

12 Then the Roman soldiers with their commanding officer and the Jewish guards arrested Jesus, tied him up, 13 and took him first to Annas. He was the father-in-law of Caiaphas, who was High Priest that year. 14 It was Caiaphas who had advised the Jewish authorities that it was better that one man should die for all the people.

Peter Denies Jesus
(Matthew 26.69, 70; Mark 14.66-68; Luke 22.55-57)

15 Simon Peter and another disciple followed Jesus. That other disciple was well known to the High Priest, so he went with Jesus into the courtyard of the High Priest's house, 16 while Peter stayed outside by the gate. Then the other disciple went back out, spoke to the girl at the gate, and brought Peter inside. 17 The girl at the gate said to Peter, "Aren't you also one of the disciples of that man?"

"No, I am not," answered Peter.

18 It was cold, so the servants and guards had built a charcoal fire and were standing around it, warming themselves. So Peter went over and stood with them, warming himself.

18.11 Mt 26.39; Mk 14.36; Lk 22.42   **18.14** Jn 11.49, 50

The High Priest Questions Jesus
(Matthew 26.59-66; Mark 14.55-64;
Luke 22.66-71)

¹⁹The High Priest questioned Jesus about his disciples and about his teaching. ²⁰Jesus answered, "I have always spoken publicly to everyone; all my teaching was done in the synagogues and in the Temple, where all the people come together. I have never said anything in secret. ²¹Why, then, do you question me? Question the people who heard me. Ask them what I told them — they know what I said."

²²When Jesus said this, one of the guards there slapped him and said, "How dare you talk like that to the High Priest!"

²³Jesus answered him, "If I have said anything wrong, tell everyone here what it was. But if I am right in what I have said, why do you hit me?"

²⁴Then Annas sent him, still tied up, to Caiaphas the High Priest.

Peter Denies Jesus Again
(Matthew 26.71-75; Mark 14.69-72;
Luke 22.58-62)

²⁵Peter was still standing there keeping himself warm. So the others said to him, "Aren't you also one of the disciples of that man?"

But Peter denied it. "No, I am not," he said.

²⁶One of the High Priest's slaves, a relative of the man whose ear Peter had cut off, spoke up. "Didn't I see you with him in the garden?" he asked.

²⁷Again Peter said "No" — and at once a rooster crowed.

Jesus before Pilate
(Matthew 27.1, 2, 11-14; Mark 15.1-5;
Luke 23.1-5)

²⁸Early in the morning Jesus was taken from Caiaphas' house to the governor's palace. The Jewish authorities did not go inside the palace, for they wanted to keep themselves ritually clean, in order to be able to eat the Passover meal. ²⁹So Pilate went outside to them and asked, "What do you accuse this man of?"

³⁰Their answer was, "We would not have brought him to you if he had not committed a crime."

³¹Pilate said to them, "Then you yourselves take him and try him according to your own law."

They replied, "We are not allowed to put anyone to death." (³²This happened in order to make come true what Jesus had said when he indicated the kind of death he would die.)

³³Pilate went back into the palace and called Jesus. "Are you the king of the Jews?" he asked him.

³⁴Jesus answered, "Does this question come from you or have others told you about me?"

³⁵Pilate replied, "Do you think I am a Jew? It was your own people and the chief priests who handed you over to me. What have you done?"

³⁶Jesus said, "My kingdom does not belong to this world; if my kingdom belonged to this world, my followers would fight to keep me from being handed over to the Jewish authorities. No, my kingdom does not belong here!"

³⁷So Pilate asked him, "Are you a king, then?"

Jesus answered, "You say that I am a king. I was born and came into the world for this one purpose, to speak about the truth. Whoever belongs to the truth listens to me."

³⁸"And what is truth?" Pilate asked.

Jesus Is Sentenced to Death
(Matthew 27.15-31; Mark 15.6-20;
Luke 23.13-25)

Then Pilate went back outside to the people and said to them, "I cannot find

18.32 Jn 3.14; 12.32

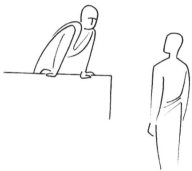

"And what is truth?" (18.38)

any reason to condemn him. ³⁹But according to the custom you have, I always set free a prisoner for you during the Passover. Do you want me to set free for you the king of the Jews?"

⁴⁰They answered him with a shout, "No, not him! We want Barabbas!" (Barabbas was a bandit.)

"No, not him! We want Barabbas!" (18.40)

19 Then Pilate took Jesus and had him whipped. ²The soldiers made a crown out of thorny branches and put it on his head; then they put a purple robe on him ³and came to him and said, "Long live the King of the Jews!" And they went up and slapped him.

⁴Pilate went back out once more and said to the crowd, "Look, I will bring him out here to you to let you see that I cannot find any reason to condemn

him." ⁵So Jesus came out, wearing the crown of thorns and the purple robe. Pilate said to them, "Look! Here is the man!"

⁶When the chief priests and the Temple guards saw him, they shouted, "Crucify him! Crucify him!"

Pilate said to them, "You take him, then, and crucify him. I find no reason to condemn him."

⁷The crowd answered back, "We have a law that says he ought to die, because he claimed to be the Son of God."

⁸When Pilate heard this, he was even more afraid. ⁹He went back into the palace and asked Jesus, "Where do you come from?"

But Jesus did not answer. ¹⁰Pilate said to him, "You will not speak to me? Remember, I have the authority to set you free and also to have you crucified."

¹¹Jesus answered, "You have authority over me only because it was given to you by God. So the man who handed me over to you is guilty of a worse sin."

¹²When Pilate heard this, he tried to find a way to set Jesus free. But the crowd shouted back, "If you set him free, that means that you are not the Emperor's friend! Anyone who claims to be a king is a rebel against the Emperor!"

¹³When Pilate heard these words, he took Jesus outside and sat down on the judge's seat in the place called "The Stone Pavement." (In Hebrew the name is "Gabbatha.") ¹⁴It was then almost noon of the day before the Passover. Pilate said to the people, "Here is your king!"

¹⁵They shouted back, "Kill him! Kill him! Crucify him!"

Pilate asked them, "Do you want me to crucify your king?"

The chief priests answered, "The only king we have is the Emperor!"

¹⁶Then Pilate handed Jesus over to them to be crucified.

Jesus Is Crucified
(Matthew 27.32-44; Mark 15.21-32;
Luke 23.26-43)

So they took charge of Jesus. ¹⁷He went out, carrying his cross, and came to "The Place of the Skull," as it is called. (In Hebrew it is called "Golgotha.") ¹⁸There they crucified him; and

He went out, carrying his cross. (19.17)

they also crucified two other men, one on each side, with Jesus between them. ¹⁹Pilate wrote a notice and had it put on the cross. "Jesus of Nazareth, the King of the Jews," is what he wrote. ²⁰Many people read it, because the place where Jesus was crucified was not far from the city. The notice was written in Hebrew, Latin, and Greek. ²¹The chief priests said to Pilate, "Do not write 'The King of the Jews,' but rather, 'This man said, I am the King of the Jews.'" ²²Pilate answered, "What I have written stays written."

²³After the soldiers had crucified Jesus, they took his clothes and divided them into four parts, one part for each soldier. They also took the robe, which was made of one piece of woven cloth without any seams in it. ²⁴The soldiers said to one another, "Let's not tear it; let's throw dice to see who will get it." This happened in order to make the scripture come true:

"They divided my clothes among themselves
and gambled for my robe."
And this is what the soldiers did.

²⁵Standing close to Jesus' cross were his mother, his mother's sister, Mary the wife of Clopas, and Mary Magdalene. ²⁶Jesus saw his mother and the disciple he loved standing there; so he said to his mother, "He is your son." ²⁷Then he said to the disciple, "She is your mother." From that time the disciple took her to live in his home.

The Death of Jesus
(Matthew 27.45-56; Mark 15.33-41;
Luke 23.44-49)

²⁸Jesus knew that by now everything had been completed; and in order to make the scripture come true, he said, "I am thirsty."

²⁹A bowl was there, full of cheap wine; so a sponge was soaked in the wine, put on a stalk of hyssop, and lifted up to his lips. ³⁰Jesus drank the wine and said, "It is finished!"

Then he bowed his head and gave up his spirit.

Jesus' Side Is Pierced

³¹Then the Jewish authorities asked Pilate to allow them to break the legs of the men who had been crucified, and to take the bodies down from the crosses. They requested this because it was Friday, and they did not want the bodies to stay on the crosses on the Sabbath, since the coming Sabbath was especially holy. ³²So the soldiers went and broke the legs of the first man and then of the other man who had been crucified with Jesus. ³³But when they came to Jesus, they saw that he was already dead, so they did not break his legs. ³⁴One of the soldiers, however, plunged his spear into Jesus' side, and at once blood and water poured out. (³⁵The one who saw this happen has spoken of it,

19.24 Ps 22.18   **19.28** Ps 69.21; 22.15

so that you also may believe.*i* What he said is true, and he knows that he speaks the truth.) 36 This was done to make the scripture come true: "Not one of his bones will be broken." 37 And there is another scripture that says, "People will look at him whom they pierced."

The Burial of Jesus
(Matthew 27.57-61; Mark 15.42-47; Luke 23.50-56)

38 After this, Joseph, who was from the town of Arimathea, asked Pilate if he could take Jesus' body. (Joseph was a follower of Jesus, but in secret, because he was afraid of the Jewish authorities.) Pilate told him he could have the body, so Joseph went and took it away. 39 Nicodemus, who at first had gone to see Jesus at night, went with Joseph, taking with him about one hundred pounds of spices, a mixture of myrrh and aloes. 40 The two men took Jesus' body and wrapped it in linen cloths with the spices according to the Jewish custom of preparing a body for

The two men took Jesus' body. (19.40)

burial. 41 There was a garden in the place where Jesus had been put to death, and in it there was a new tomb where no one had ever been buried.

42 Since it was the day before the Sabbath and because the tomb was close by, they placed Jesus' body there.

The Empty Tomb
(Matthew 28.1-8; Mark 16.1-8; Luke 24.1-12)

20 Early on Sunday morning, while it was still dark, Mary Magdalene went to the tomb and saw that the stone had been taken away from the entrance. 2 She went running to Simon Peter and the other disciple, whom Jesus loved, and told them, "They have taken the Lord from the tomb, and we don't know where they have put him!"

3 Then Peter and the other disciple went to the tomb. 4 The two of them were running, but the other disciple ran faster than Peter and reached the tomb first. 5 He bent over and saw the linen cloths, but he did not go in. 6 Behind him came Simon Peter, and he went straight into the tomb. He saw the linen cloths lying there 7 and the cloth which had been around Jesus' head. It was not lying with the linen cloths but was rolled up by itself. 8 Then the other disciple, who had reached the tomb first, also went in; he saw and believed. (9 They still did not understand the scripture which said that he must rise from death.) 10 Then the disciples went back home.

Jesus Appears to Mary Magdalene
(Matthew 28.9, 10; Mark 16.9-11)

11 Mary stood crying outside the tomb. While she was still crying, she bent over and looked in the tomb 12 and saw two angels there dressed in white, sitting where the body of Jesus had been, one at the head and the other at

---

i believe; *some manuscripts have* continue to believe.
19.36 Ex 12.46; Nu 9.12; Ps 34.20   **19.37** Zec 12.10; Rev 1.7   **19.39** Jn 3.1, 2

the feet. [13]"Woman, why are you crying?" they asked her.

She answered, "They have taken my Lord away, and I do not know where they have put him!"

[14]Then she turned around and saw Jesus standing there; but she did not know that it was Jesus. [15]"Woman, why are you crying?" Jesus asked her. "Who is it that you are looking for?"

She thought he was the gardener, so she said to him, "If you took him away, sir, tell me where you have put him, and I will go and get him."

[16]Jesus said to her, "Mary!"

She turned toward him and said in Hebrew, "Rabboni!" (This means "Teacher.")

[17]"Do not hold on to me," Jesus told her, "because I have not yet gone back up to the Father. But go to my brothers and tell them that I am returning to him who is my Father and their Father, my God and their God."

[18]So Mary Magdalene went and told the disciples that she had seen the Lord and related to them what he had told her.

Jesus Appears to His Disciples
(Matthew 28.16-20; Mark 16.14-18; Luke 24.36-49)

[19]It was late that Sunday evening, and the disciples were gathered together behind locked doors, because they were afraid of the Jewish authorities. Then Jesus came and stood among them. "Peace be with you," he said. [20]After saying this, he showed them his hands and his side. The disciples were filled with joy at seeing the Lord. [21]Jesus said to them again, "Peace be with you. As the Father sent me, so I send you." [22]Then he breathed on them and said, "Receive the Holy Spirit. [23]If you forgive people's sins, they are forgiven; if you do not forgive them, they are not forgiven."

Jesus and Thomas

[24]One of the twelve disciples, Thomas (called the Twin), was not with them when Jesus came. [25]So the other disciples told him, "We have seen the Lord!"

Thomas said to them, "Unless I see the scars of the nails in his hands and put my finger on those scars and my hand in his side, I will not believe."

[26]A week later the disciples were together again indoors, and Thomas was with them. The doors were locked, but Jesus came and stood among them and said, "Peace be with you." [27]Then he said to Thomas, "Put your finger here, and look at my hands; then reach out your hand and put it in my side. Stop your doubting, and believe!"

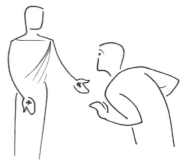

"Look at my hands. . . . Stop your doubting, and believe!" (20.27)

[28]Thomas answered him, "My Lord and my God!"

[29]Jesus said to him, "Do you believe because you see me? How happy are those who believe without seeing me!"

The Purpose of This Book

[30]In his disciples' presence Jesus performed many other miracles which are not written down in this book. [31]But these have been written in order that you may believe [i] that Jesus is the

---

[i] believe; *some manuscripts have* continue to believe.
20.23 Mt 16.19; 18.18

Messiah, the Son of God, and that through your faith in him you may have life.

Jesus Appears to Seven Disciples

21 After this, Jesus appeared once more to his disciples at Lake Tiberias. This is how it happened. ²Simon Peter, Thomas (called the Twin), Nathanael (the one from Cana in Galilee), the sons of Zebedee, and two other disciples of Jesus were all together. ³Simon Peter said to the others, "I am going fishing."

"We will come with you," they told him. So they went out in a boat, but all that night they did not catch a thing. ⁴As the sun was rising, Jesus stood at the water's edge, but the disciples did not know that it was Jesus. ⁵Then he asked them, "Young men, haven't you caught anything?"

"Not a thing," they answered.

⁶He said to them, "Throw your net out on the right side of the boat, and you will catch some." So they threw the net out and could not pull it back in, because they had caught so many fish.

⁷The disciple whom Jesus loved said to Peter, "It is the Lord!" When Peter heard that it was the Lord, he wrapped his outer garment around him (for he had taken his clothes off) and jumped into the water. ⁸The other disciples came to shore in the boat, pulling the net full of fish. They were not very far from land, about a hundred yards away. ⁹When they stepped ashore, they saw a charcoal fire there with fish on it and some bread. ¹⁰Then Jesus said to them, "Bring some of the fish you have just caught."

¹¹Simon Peter went aboard and dragged the net ashore full of big fish, a hundred and fifty-three in all; even though there were so many, still the net did not tear. ¹²Jesus said to them, "Come and eat." None of the disciples

Simon Peter . . . dragged the net ashore. (21.11)

dared ask him, "Who are you?" because they knew it was the Lord. ¹³So Jesus went over, took the bread, and gave it to them; he did the same with the fish.

¹⁴This, then, was the third time Jesus appeared to the disciples after he was raised from death.

Jesus and Peter

¹⁵After they had eaten, Jesus said to Simon Peter, "Simon son of John, do you love me more than these others do?"

"Yes, Lord," he answered, "you know that I love you."

Jesus said to him, "Take care of my lambs." ¹⁶A second time Jesus said to him, "Simon son of John, do you love me?"

"Yes, Lord," he answered, "you know that I love you."

Jesus said to him, "Take care of my sheep." ¹⁷A third time Jesus said, "Simon son of John, do you love me?"

Peter became sad because Jesus asked him the third time, "Do you love me?" and so he said to him, "Lord, you know everything; you know that I love you!"

Jesus said to him, "Take care of my

21.3 Lk 5.5   21.6 Lk 5.6

sheep. [18] I am telling you the truth: when you were young, you used to get ready and go anywhere you wanted to; but when you are old, you will stretch out your hands and someone else will tie you up and take you where you don't want to go." [19] (In saying this, Jesus was indicating the way in which Peter would die and bring glory to God.) Then Jesus said to him, "Follow me!"

Jesus and the Other Disciple

[20] Peter turned around and saw behind him that other disciple, whom Jesus loved — the one who had leaned close to Jesus at the meal and had asked, "Lord, who is going to betray you?" [21] When Peter saw him, he asked Jesus, "Lord, what about this man?"

21.20 Jn 13.25

[22] Jesus answered him, "If I want him to live until I come, what is that to you? Follow me!"

[23] So a report spread among the followers of Jesus that this disciple would not die. But Jesus did not say he would not die; he said, "If I want him to live until I come, what is that to you?"

[24] He is the disciple who spoke of these things, the one who also wrote them down; and we know that what he said is true.

Conclusion

[25] Now, there are many other things that Jesus did. If they were all written down one by one, I suppose that the whole world could not hold the books that would be written.

WORD LIST

This Word List identifies many objects or cultural features whose meaning may not be known to all readers.

Abyss The place in the depths of the earth where the demons were imprisoned until their final punishment.

Agate A semiprecious stone of various colors, but usually white and brown.

Alabaster A soft stone of usually light creamy color, from which vases and jars were made.

Aloes A sweet-smelling substance, derived from a plant. It was used medicinally and as a perfume.

Amen A Hebrew word which means "it is so" or "may it be so." It can also be translated "certainly," "truly," or "surely." In Revelation 3.14 it is used as a title for Christ.

Amethyst A semiprecious stone, usually purple or violet in color.

Anoint To pour or rub olive oil on someone in order to honor him or to appoint him to some special work. The Israelite kings were anointed as a sign of their taking office, and so the king could be called "the anointed one." In a figurative sense, "The Anointed One" is the title of the one whom God chose and appointed as Savior and Lord.

Apostle Principally one of the group of twelve men whom Jesus chose to be his special followers and helpers. It is also used in the New Testament to refer to Paul and other Christians workers. The word may have the sense of "messenger."

Areopagus A hill in Athens where the city council used to meet. For this reason the council itself was called Areopagus, even after it no longer met on the hill.

Artemis The Greek name of an ancient goddess of fertility, worshiped especially in Asia Minor.

Baal The god of fertility worshiped by the Canaanites; his female counterpart was Asherah. After the Hebrews invaded Canaan, many of them began worshiping these two gods.

Barley A cultivated grain similar to wheat, grown as a food crop.

Beelzebul A New Testament name given to the Devil as the chief of the evil spirits.

Beryl A semiprecious stone usually green or bluish green in color.

Breastplate Part of a soldier's armor, made of leather or metal; it covered the chest and sometimes the back as a protection against arrows and the blows of a sword.

Carnelian A semiprecious stone, usually red in color.

Chalcedony A semiprecious stone, usually milky or gray in color.

Christ Originally a title, the Greek equivalent of the Hebrew word "Messiah." It means "the anointed one." Jesus was called the Christ because he was the one whom God chose and sent as Savior and Lord.

Circumcise To cut off the foreskin of the penis. As a sign of God's covenant with his people Israelite boys were circumcised eight days after they were born (Genesis 17.9-14).

Council The supreme religious court of the Jews, composed of seventy leaders of the Jewish people and presided over by the High Priest.

Covenant An agreement, either between persons or between God and a person or a people.

Covenant Box The wooden chest covered with gold, in which were kept the two stone tablets on which were written the Ten Commandments. It has traditionally been called the Ark of the Covenant.

Cumin A small plant whose seeds are ground up and used for seasoning foods.

Dedication, Festival of The Jewish festival, lasting eights days, which celebrated the restoration and rededication in 165 B.C. of the Temple altar by the Jewish patriot Judas Maccabeus. The festival began on the 25th day of the month Kislev (around December 10). The Jewish name for this festival is Hanukkah.

Defile To make ritually unclean or impure. Certain foods and practices were prohibited by the Law of Moses because they were thought to make a person ritually or ceremonially unclean. Such persons could not take part in the public worship until they had performed certain rituals which would remove the defilement.

Demon An evil spirit with the power to harm people; it was regarded as a messenger and servant of the Devil.

Dill A small garden plant whose stems, leaves, and seed are used for seasoning food.

Disciple A person who follows and learns from someone else. In the New Testament the word used of the followers of John the Baptist and especially of the followers of Jesus, particularly the twelve apostles.

Dragon A legendary beast, thought to be like a huge lizard. It is also called a serpent and appears as a figure of the Devil (Revelation 12.3−13.4; 20.2,3).

Elders In the Old Testament this is a name given to certain respected leaders of a tribe, nation, or city. In the New Testament three different groups are called elders: (1) in the Gospels the elders are influential Jewish religious leaders, some of whom were members of the supreme Council; (2) in Acts 11−21 and the Letters the elders are Christian church officers who had general responsibility for the work of the church; (3) in Revelation the twenty-four elders are part of God's court in heaven, perhaps as representatives of God's people.

Epicureans Those who followed the teaching of Epicurus (died 270 B.C.), a Greek philosopher who taught that happiness is the highest good in life.

Epileptic A person who suffers from a nervous disease causing convulsions and fainting.

Eunuch A man who has been made physically incapable of having normal sexual relations. Eunuchs were often important officials in the court of ancient kings, and the term may have come to be used of such officials in general, regardless of their sexual condition.

Fast To go without food for a while as a religious duty.

Frankincense A valuable incense made from the sap of a certain tree. This incense was probably imported from Arabia.

Gentile A person who is not a Jew.

Hades The Greek name used in the New Testament to refer to the world of the dead.

Harvest Festival The Israelite festival celebrating the wheat harvest, held in the latter part of May, fifty days after Passover. The Jewish name for this festival is Shavuoth (The Feast of Weeks). It has also been called Pentecost.

Hermes The name of a Greek god who served as messenger of the gods.

Herod's party A political party in New Testament times composed of Jews who favored being ruled by one of the descendants of Herod the Great rather than by the Roman governor.

High Priest The priest who occupied the highest office in the Jewish priestly system and was president of the supreme Council of the Jews. Once a year (on the Day of Atonement) he would enter the Most Holy Place in the Temple and offer sacrifice for himself and for the sins of the people of Israel.

Hyssop A small bushy plant, used in religious ceremonies to sprinkle liquids.

Incense Material which is burned in order to produce a pleasant smell. The Israelites used it in their worship.

Jasper A semiprecious stone of various colors. The jasper mentioned in the Bible was probably green, or else clear.

Law The name that the Jews applied to the first five books of the Old Testament, also called "The Books of Moses." Sometimes, however, the name is applied in a more general way to the entire Old Testament.

Levite (1) A member of the tribe of Levi; (2) a man who assisted the priest in the performance of religious duties.

Living creatures (also referred to as "winged creatures" and traditionally called "cherubim") Symbols of God's majesty and associated with his presence. For a description of such creatures see Exodus 25.18-20; Ezekiel 1.5-13; 10; Revelation 4.6-9.

Manna A food eaten by the Israelites during their travels in the wilderness. It was white and flaky and looked like small seeds (Exodus 16.14-21; Numbers 11.7-9)

Messiah A Hebrew title (meaning "the anointed one") given to the promised Savior, whose coming was foretold by the Hebrew prophets; the corresponding Greek term "The Christ" has the same meaning.

Most Holy Place The innermost room of the Tent of the Lord's presence or the Temple. The Covenant Box was kept there. Only the High Priest could enter the Most Holy Place, and he did so only once a year, on the Day of Atonement.

Mustard A large plant which grows from a very small seed. The seeds were ground into powder and used as spice on food.

Myrrh A sweet-smelling resin that was highly priced. It served as a medicine (Mark 15.23) and was used by the Jews to prepare bodies for burial (John 19.39).

Nard An expensive perfume made from a plant.

Nazarene Someone from the town of Nazareth. The name was used as a title for Jesus and also as a name for early Christians (Acts 24.5).

New Moon Festival A religious observance held by the Israelites on the day of each new moon.

Onyx A semiprecious stone of various colors.

Outcasts In the Gospels this name, which in many translations appears as "sinners," refers to those Jews who had been excluded from synagogue worship because they violated rules about foods that should not be eaten and about associating with people who were not Jews. Such outcasts were despised by many of their fellow Jews, and Jesus was criticized for associating with them (Mark 2.15-17; Luke 7.34; 15.1,2).

Parable A story which teaches spiritual truth; such stories were often used by Jesus.

Paradise A name for heaven (Luke 23.43; 2 Corinthians 12.3).

Paralytic Someone who suffers from a disease that prevents him from moving part or all of his body.

Passover The Israelite festival, on the 14th day of the month Nisan (around April 1), which celebrated the deliverance of the ancient Hebrews from their captivity in Egypt. The Angel of Death killed the first-born in the Egyptian homes but passed over the Hebrew homes (Exodus 12.23-27). The Jewish name for this festival is Pesach.

Pentecost, Day of The Greek name for the Israelite festival of wheat harvest (see Harvest Festival). The name Pentecost (meaning "fiftieth") comes from the fact that the feast was held fifty days after Passover.

Pharisees A Jewish religious party during the time of Jesus. They were strict in obeying the Law of Moses and other religious regulations which had been added to it through the centuries.

Preparation, Day of The sixth day of the week (Friday), on which the Jews made the required preparations to observe the Sabbath (Saturday).

Prophet A person who proclaims a message from God. The term usually refers to certain prophets in the Old Testament, but the New Testament speaks of prophets in the early church. John the Baptist is also called a prophet.

Quartz A semiprecious stone of various colors, but usually clear.

Rabbi A Hebrew word which means "my teacher."

Red Sea Evidently referred originally to (1) a series of lakes and marshes between the head of the Gulf of Suez and the Mediterranean, the region generally regarded as the site of the events described in Exodus 13, and was also used to designate (2) the Gulf of Suez, (3) the Gulf of Aqaba.

Rephan The name of an ancient god that was worshiped as the ruler of the planet Saturn.

Sabbath The seventh day of the Jewish week (from sundown on Friday to sundown on Saturday), a holy day in which no work was permitted.

Sackcloth A coarse cloth made of goats' hair, which was worn as a sign of mourning or distress.

Sadducees A small Jewish religious party in New Testament times, composed largely of priests. They based their beliefs primarily on the first five books of the Old Testament and differed in several matters of belief and practice from the larger party of the Pharisees.

Samaritan A name used to refer to a native of Samaria, the region between Judea and Galilee. Because of differences in politics, race, customs, and religion (including especially the central place of worship), there was much bad feeling between the Jews and the Samaritans.

Sapphire A very valuable stone, usually blue in color.

Scorpion A small creature which has eight legs and a long tail with a poisonous sting. It can inflict a very painful, and sometimes fatal, wound.

Scriptures In the New Testament the word refers to the collected body of Hebrew sacred writings, known to Christians as the Old Testament. Various names are used: the Law (or the Law of Moses) and the prophets (Matthew 5.17; Luke 2.22; 24.44; Act 13.15; 28.23); the Holy Scriptures (Romans 1.2; 2 Timothy 3.15); the old covenant (2 Corinthians 3.14). The singular "scripture" refers to a single passage of the Old Testament.

Serpent A name given to the dragon which appears in the New Testament as a figure of the Devil (Revelation 12.3-17; 20.2,3).

Shelters, Festival of A joyous festival celebrated by the Israelites in the fall after the completion of the harvest. In order to make them remember the years when their ancestors wandered through the wilderness, the Israelites constructed enough shelters to live in during the festival. The Jewish name for this festival is Sukkoth. It has been traditionally called the Feast of Tabernacles or the Feast of Booths.

Sickle A tool consisting of a curved metal blade and a wooden handle used for cutting wheat and other crops.

Stoics Those who followed the teachings of the Greek philosopher Zeno (died 265 B.C.), who taught that happiness is to be found in being free from pleasure and pain.

Sulfur In the Bible this refers to a sulfur compound which burns with great heat and produces an unpleasant smell.

Synagogue A place where Jews met every Sabbath day for their public worship. It probably also served as a center for Jewish social life and a school for Jewish children.

Teachers of the Law Men who in New Testament times taught and interpreted the teachings of the Old Testament, especially the first five books.

Tenant A person who grows crops on land owned by someone else, and turns over a part of the harvest to the owner to pay for the use of that land.

Topaz A semiprecious stone, usually yellow in color.

Turquoise A semiprecious stone, blue or bluish green in color.

Unleavened Bread, Festival of The Israelite festival, lasting seven days after Passover; it also celebrated the deliverance of the ancient Hebrews from Egypt. The name came from the practice of not using leaven (yeast) in making the bread during that week (Exodus 12.14-20). It was held from the 15th to the 22nd day of the month Nisan (around the first week of April).

Vow A strong declaration or promise, usually made while calling upon God to punish the speaker if the statement should prove to be not true or if the promise were not kept.

Winged creatures (also referred to as "living creatures" and traditionally called "cherubim") Symbol of God's majesty and associated with his presence. For a description of such creatures see Exodus 25.18-20; Ezekiel 1.5-13; Revelation 4.6-9.

Winnowing shovel A tool like a shovel or a large fork, used to separate the wheat from the chaff.

Wreath Flowers or leaves arranged in a circle, to be placed on a person's head. In ancient times a wreath of leaves was the prize given to winners in athletic contests.

Yeast A substance, also called leaven, which is added to dough made from the flour of wheat or barley to make it rise before being baked into bread.

Yoke A heavy bar of wood fitted over the necks of two oxen to make it possible for them to pull a plow or a cart. The word is used figuratively to describe the moral lessons that a teacher passes on to pupils.

Zeus The name of the supreme god of the Greeks.

Zion Originally a designation for "David's City," the Jebusite stronghold captured by King David's forces. The term "Zion" was later extended in meaning to refer to the hill on which the Temple stood.

PISIDIA

Antioch

Iconium

Lystra

Derbe

CILICIA

Tarsus

Attalia PAMPHYLIA

LYCIA Perga

Patara

Myra

CYPRUS

Salamis

Paphos

Seleucia

Antioch

SYRIA

Euphrates R.

MEDITERRANEAN

SEA

PHOENICIA

Sidon

Tyre

Ptolemais

Caesarea

Joppa

Azotus

Gaza

JUDEA

Samaria

Lydda

Jerusalem

Damascus

PALESTINE AND SYRIA

0 Miles 200

0 Kms 200

Alexandria

© United Bible Societies, 1976

PALESTINE IN THE TIME OF JESUS

Miles
0   40

Kms
0   40

MEDITERRANEAN

SEA

PHOENICIA

LEBANON MTS.

SYRIA

Abila
ABILENE
Damascus

Sidon

Zarephath

▲ *MT. HERMON*

Tyre

• Caesarea Philippi

Ptolemais

GALILEE
Chorazin
Capernaum • • Bethsaida
Magadan   *Lake*
Cana   Tiberias   *Galilee*
• Nazareth

MT. CARMEL ▲

▲ *MT.*
TABOR
Nain •   • Gadara

Caesarea

TEN TOWNS

Salim
Aenon
SAMARIA

Samaria
•

MT. EBAL
MT. GERIZIM ▲ ▲ Sychar

• Gerasa

P
E
R
E
A

Jordan River

Joppa

Arimathea?

Ephraim •

Jericho • • Bethany

Emmaus •
Jerusalem • • Bethany
Azotus •   Qumran

Ascalon

J U D E A   Bethlehem

Gaza   • Hebron

Dead

Sea

I D U M E A

N
A
B
A
T
E
A

© United Bible Societies, 1976

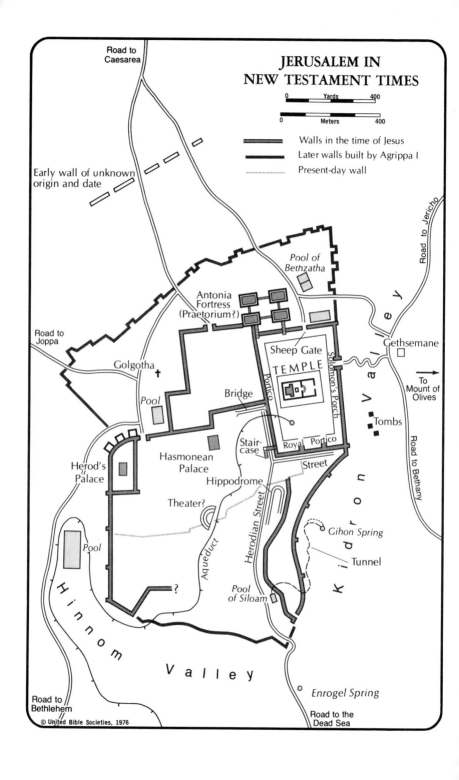

JERUSALEM IN NEW TESTAMENT TIMES

0   Yards   400

0   Meters   400

Walls in the time of Jesus

Later walls built by Agrippa I

Present-day wall

Road to Caesarea

Early wall of unknown origin and date

Road to Jericho

Pool of Bethzatha

Antonia Fortress (Praetorium?)

Road to Joppa

Golgotha

Sheep Gate

TEMPLE

Solomon's Porch

Gethsemane

To Mount of Olives

Pool

Bridge

Portico

Tombs

Staircase

Royal Portico

Street

Hasmonean Palace

Herod's Palace

Hippodrome

Theater?

Herodian Street

Aqueduct

Road to Bethany

Gihon Spring

Tunnel

Pool

?

Pool of Siloam

K i d r o n   V a l l e y

H i n n o m   V a l l e y

Road to Bethlehem

© United Bible Societies, 1976

Enrogel Spring

Road to the Dead Sea